q

VIATION, INC.

............13 FT 2 1/8 IN.

............8 FT 8 IN.

KARD "MERLIN" V-1650
5HP V-12 ENGINE

AGE CROSS SECTIONS

SECTION C-C   SECTION D-D   SECTION E-E

ABILIZER OFFSET

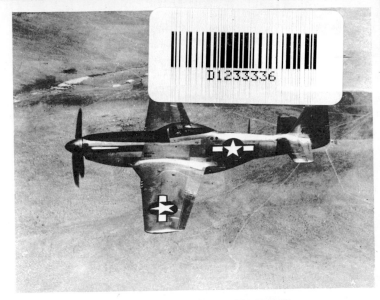

U.S. ARMY AIR FORCE P-51D 'MUSTANG'

NORTH AMERICAN AVIATION, INC

Rated the best of the World War II fighters, the P-51 Mustangs returned to combat during the Korean War and concluded active service with National Guard and Reserve squadrons. These are the airplanes that "broke the back" of the Luftwaffe when in 1944 they began flying long-range escort missions over Berlin. Mainly a fighter, the Mustang also served as a fighter-bomber, a photo-reconnaissance plane, and a dive bomber. Originally designed for the British and accepted by the U.S. Army Air Force only after it had proved itself, the P-51 eventually was rated by a senate investigating committee as "the most aerodynamically perfect pursuit plane in existence." The P-51D, last of the Mustangs to be used in World War II, is shown in the accompanying drawing.

COOLANT FILLER CAP

OIL FILLER CAP

GAS FILLER CAP

DORSAL FILLET ADDED ON "D" MODELS TO COMPENSATE FOR LOSS OF KEEL SURFACE WITH BUBBLE CANOPY.

414214

ENGINE VENT

WHIP ANTENNA

FLIGHT VIEW

ANTI-GLARE PANEL

A   B   C   D   E

1° 45 MIN.

FUSELAGE

THRUST

414214

F

G

FUSELAGE REFERENCE PLANE

OIL RADIATOR SHUTTER "OPEN"

ENGINE COOLANT RADIATOR SHUTTER "OPEN"

E

A   B   C   D

SIDE VIEW

AIRPLANE ₵

ODER

0 1 2 3 4 5 6 7 8 9 10

SCALE IN FEET

NA-62-1494

U.S. ARMY AIR FORCE

P-51D *Mustang*

FIGHTER

DESIGNED AND BUILT BY NORTH AMERICAN AVIATION, INC

SCALE: NOTED   1/74 TH   DATE: DECEMBER 1962

PREPARED BY NORTH AMERICAN AVIATION, INC.

FIGHTING MUSTANG: THE CHRONICLE OF THE P-51

Fighting

A flight of Mustangs from the 374th Fighter Squadron, 361st Fighter Group in line abreast formation. (USAF)

Mustang

THE CHRONICLE OF THE P-51

by William N. Hess

Doubleday & Company, Inc.,
Garden City, New York

DEDICATED TO

THE MUSTANG PILOTS

Library of Congress Catalog Card Number 72–102786
Copyright © 1970 by William N. Hess
All Rights Reserved. Printed in the United States of America
9 8 7 6 5 4 3

ACKNOWLEDGMENTS

MANY YEARS of intensive research in the field of fighter planes and aces spawned the idea for this book. The encouragement of Mr. Stanley M. Ulanoff, more research and many people have made it possible.

Lt. Col. Robert A. Webb, Chief, Book Branch of the Office of the Assistant Secretary of Defense, opened the doors to the official records, and Miss Margo Kennedy and the wonderful staff of Aerospace Studies Institute left no stone unturned to make these records available to me.

Mr. J. L. Typer and Mr. D. B. Wright of North American Rockwell Corporation dug deeply into the records at the home of the Mustang to make them available. Mr. Gerald Tyler and Cavalier Aircraft Corporation brought the history of the Mustang up to date.

Wartime Mustang pilots furnished invaluable assistance from their excellent memories of those days. To these veteran pilots my heartfelt thanks: Lt. Col. Richard E. Turner, Ret., M/Gen. Edward B. Giller, Col. Sidney S. Woods, Ret., Dr. Clayton K. Gross, Mr. Kenneth H. Dahlberg, Mr. Jim Brooks, Mr. Fred Holmes, S/Ldr. F. E. Dymond, Mr. J. B. Walton, Jr., Mr. Wendell Hook, Col. Bert W. Marshall, Jr., Ret., Col. William T. Whisner, and Lt. Col. Robert Goebel, Ret.

Deepest appreciation to Mr. Grover C. Hall for his co-operation and assistance. My fine English aviation historians Mr. Chris Shores and Mr. Roger C. Freeman came through with vital information in their usual wonderful manner.

Many of the excellent and rare photos in this book came from private collections. The generosity of these men is unexcelled: Mr. R. C. Jones, Mr. Richard M. Hill, Mr. Albert H. Meryman, T/Sgt. David W. Menard, Mr. Ernie McDowell, Mr. Robert M. Gers, Mr. David Weatherill, Mr. Kenn C. Rust, Mr. Ralph R. Howard and Mr. Earl Reinert.

Finally, to my wife Ann, my deepest gratitude for her patience through the trials and tribulations of putting these pages together.

CONTENTS

CHAPTER 1

THE COLT

THE Mustang does not owe its birth to the U. S. Army Air Force with which it gained its greatest fame. It cannot be said that its conception was made possible by the British Air Purchasing Commission. This design became reality due to the foresight and determination of one man—James H. "Dutch" Kindelberger.

As early as 1938, Kindelberger had made numerous trips to Europe seeking aircraft orders for his young North American Aviation Company, and there he had the opportunity to see and observe the airplanes which would see their initial combat action in 1939. After hostilities broke out in Europe, Kindelberger eagerly sought out reports of aircraft performance from observers in the combat arena. From this information, ideas of his own were developed that would bear lasting benefits to the Allies in the years to come.

In April of 1940, Kindelberger was summoned by the British Air Purchasing Commission and requested to put into production in his plant the Curtiss P-40 for use by the Royal Air Force.

Well aware of the limitations of the P-40 and anxious to put his own ideas into action, Kindelberger replied, "Hell, we can do better than that airplane and design you a real one in the same time it will take to put this thing in production."

There were serious doubts expressed, but the British were willing to give him the opportunity. Kindelberger returned to his plant in California, and showing great faith in his design team, presented them with the challenge. Edgar Schmued and Raymond Rice went to work immediately to come up with a prototype. Relying heavily on the axiom, "You can't pull a rabbit out of a hat unless you carefully put a rabbit into the hat beforehand," Kindelberger demanded the best from his engineers and he got it. Customary design procedure was forgotten. Design data was immediately rushed to

The original Mustang. NA-73, the prototype of the P-51. (NORTH AMERICAN)

men who were preparing the wooden mock-up of the airplane in the experimental shop. A $20,000 laminated-mahogany scale model was prepared for wind-tunnel tests in record time, yet tolerances were measured down to .001 of an inch.

In a drab room over Kindelberger's office the design team knew no hours. The lights never went out and the average day was at least sixteen hours long.

Several innovations marked the design for success. One was the laminar flow wing which, with its maximum thickness well aft, resulted in greatly reduced drag which in turn made possible greater speed for given horsepower. The National Advisory Committee for Aeronautics had developed this high-lift, low-drag airfoil, but most engineers were of the opinion that it was too revolutionary and unproved to be incorporated into a mass-produced aircraft. North American's team decided to give it a try, but promised to come up with a conventional wing within thirty days should the test fail.

When the first wind-tunnel tests were run on the wing at California Institute of Technology, it seemed that the laminar flow wing had not lived up to expectations. Stalling characteristics were bad. Quickly and carefully the airfoil was modified and brought back, but once again the wing didn't check out satisfactorily. Then the engineers suspected that the model was too large for the tunnel; the walls were affecting the airflow at the wing tips. The model was then taken by plane to the University of Washington at Seattle where a larger tunnel was available. Here the wing passed all its tests with flying colors!

The radiator for the Allison engine was positioned aft of the cockpit with a further drag-eliminating narrow intake. Here, too, difficulties were encountered as turbulence tended to build up under the wing, which prevented a clean flow of air into the scoop. This was remedied by dropping the entrance an inch. This proved sufficient enough to bypass the disturbed air under the wing. Once this was accomplished, the design enjoyed the smallest and most drag-free cross-sectional area placed behind any American-built inline engine.

North American further differentiated from all other Allied designers in incorporating square wing tips and tail surfaces. From the first day forward, the Mustang truly possessed the lines of a champion.

Delay in the delivery of the Allison V-1710-39 engine prevented the first flight from being made until October 26, 1940, although the prototype was rolled out on borrowed wheels in approximately 125 days. Test pilot Vance Breese took the shiny new aircraft designated NA-73S into the blue that fall day and is reported to have thought highly of its performance. The Colt was born!

The first production NA-73 was retained at North American for testing purposes, but the second craft went to England for testing where it arrived in November of 1941. Here it was dubbed the Mustang Mark I. This new fighter gained quick recognition as the best aircraft yet to be delivered from America, although it was handicapped by its low-altitude-rated Allison engine. On the other hand, it was highly maneuverable, and its internal fuel capacity of 150 imperial gallons of fuel gave it a range potential far surpassing that of any fighters on duty with the Royal Air Force. It possessed a heavy armament load of four .50-caliber and two

A Mustang Mark I showing K-24 camera installation behind cockpit.
(RAF OFFICIAL)

Mustang Mark I of 26 Squadron RAF. Note solid camera port aft of cockpit.
(SMITH *via* JONES)

.30-caliber machine guns which provided great strafing capability. These features suggested its use for tactical reconnaissance and ground support.

On the strength of its performance in the testing program, the first British contract was let calling for the delivery of 320 of the new fighters with the proviso that two of the machines be delivered to the U. S. Army Air Corps for evaluation. These two aircraft, being the fifth and tenth production NA-73s, were designated XP-51s.

The Mustangs delivered under the original contract differed little from the original model other than that an F-24 camera had been mounted behind the pilot. It was in a ground-support configuration that the Mustang entered service with the Royal Air Force Army Co-operation Squadrons.

The first unit to receive the aircraft was No. 26 Squadron which began augmenting their Curtiss Tomahawks with the new fighter in February 1942. In April, two more squadrons were so equipped and a further eight squadrons received Mustang Is during June.

No. 26 Squadron took the Mustang I on its first operational sortie on July 27, 1942, but it was during the Dieppe landings by British commandos on August 19, 1942, that the fighter received its baptism of fire. On this day, pilots of No. 414 RCAF Squadron were attacked over the port city by FW 190s. During this fight, F/O H. H. Hills downed one of the enemy. First blood for the Mustang!

RAF Mustang Mark I of Army Co-operation on typical low-level flight. (USAF)

A Mustang Mark I which operated with 2 Squadron RAF during 1942–44.
(COOK *via* JONES)

On the same day, P/O C. H. Stover, while flying wingman on a deep reconnaissance, was attacked by a low-flying Focke-Wulf. In the course of violent evasive action on the deck, Stover ran into a telephone pole and lost three feet from the tip of his starboard wing. Despite this, he managed to bring the Mustang home to England where he made a crash landing.

The first announcement of the long-range capability of the Mustang appeared in English newspapers during October of 1942 and read as follows: "The Mustangs—American-built and the fastest co-operational aircraft in the world—had for their targets the Dortmund-Ems Canal and objectives in Holland. They made a round trip of between 600 and 700 miles . . ."

On this mission the Mustang I became the first single-engined fighter based in the United Kingdom to penetrate the German border. The Mustangs opened their attack just before crossing the German-Dutch frontier when they machine gunned a military camp while flying right down on the deck. Then, in the Dortmund-Ems Canal, they swept down on a factory and gas depot at Lathen. Continuing along the canal, they scored hits on several barges and left a 500-ton ship burning in the Zuyder Zee.

The Royal Air Force was so pleased with the Mustang I that it placed an order for 300 more of the craft which embodied only minor modifications. Subsequently another 150 fighters were ordered which called for the machine guns to be replaced by four 20-mm cannon. This was in keeping with the

A Mustang Mark IA of the Royal Air Force. Note the installation of 20-mm guns in the wings. (RCAF)

Royal Air Force policy at that time which was attempting to increase the firepower of its fighters. These cannon-carrying craft were designated NA-91 by North American and Mustang Mark IA by the Royal Air Force.

However, the British never received all of the aircraft manufactured under this contract for 150 Mustangs. Fifty-five NA-91s were delivered to the U. S. Army Air Force armed with four .50-caliber machine guns rather than cannon and fitted with two K-24 cameras. These aircraft were designated

Experimental Mustang Mark I fitted with the Merlin 65 engine during testing over England. The circle "P" denotes prototype. (RUST)

as tactical reconnaissance planes and were typed F-6As by the Army
Air Force. The planes were originally code named Apache, but this Indian
tribal name didn't stick and in only a few months the United States forces
chose to call the aircraft by its British title—Mustang. A number of the
F-6As saw action in North Africa during the Tunisian campaign.

At the time of testing the Mustang in Great Britain, Maj. Thomas
Hitchcock was serving as the U. S. Military Attaché in London and this
veteran pilot was swept up with the early success and performance of the
aircraft. In the fall of 1942 he informed Washington that the Mustang was
by far the best fighter airframe developed to date, but in view of the short-
coming of the Allison engine, he proposed a marriage of the North American
airframe with the Rolls-Royce Merlin 61 engine. His opinion was seconded
by others including Royal Air Force Air Marshal Sir Stafford Leigh-Mallory.
Four Mustangs were delivered to the Rolls-Royce factory for modification.

A Mustang Mark I received a Merlin 65 and a Mustang IA was
modified to take a Merlin 61 and both were fitted with four-bladed propellers.
During the testing, a further two airplanes were fitted with Merlins and
were designated Mustang Xs. The flight tests were amazing and so impressed

The RAF utilized many Mustang Is for photo reconnaissance.
This camera-equipped craft belonged to No. 2 Squadron. (COOK *via* JONES)

all concerned that North American saw fit to initiate redesigning the aircraft to take the Packard-built Merlin, the V-1650-3, with two-speed, two-stage supercharger and intercooler.

Two P-51s were equipped with the Packard-built engines at the California plant for testing and for a time carried the designation of XP-78s, but this soon gave way to XP-51B. The airframes were beefed up, the carburetor intake was moved from above to below the nose and underwing racks were installed to take two 1000-pound bombs or long-range fuel drop tanks.

The high-altitude performance and increase in level speed of the new Mustang to 441 mph were enough to really sell the USAAF on the little fighter, and an initial order of 2200 Merlin-powered P-51Bs was placed with North American.

Meanwhile, pilots of the Royal Air Force Co-operation Command continued to do yeoman duty over occupied countries of Europe. Bombing, strafing and tactical reconnaissance comprised the bulk of their missions. A favorite with the pilots was train busting. A young South African pilot reported, "I flew over one engine pulling thirty cars and gave it a squirt. Then I went on down the line, got another just about to go under a bridge. The engine did not burst, but it was just as if you had put a lot of holes suddenly in a tin can. Steam blew all over the place."

Such activities placed quite a strain on the German-operated railroads. Engines had to be armored and flak guns were placed on flatcars, but the measures were never enough. During this period of time, passenger trains were strictly "taboo" due to the large number of friendly civilians occupying the coaches, but if a pilot got a good crack at the locomotive, the train was apt to run late.

Royal Air Force pilots were not only pleased with the excellent performance of the Mustang, but with its ability to take punishment and come home. "The sturdiness of these splendid U.S. fighters is wonderful," one British pilot testified. "Some of them have taken punishment which would have been too much for most fighters. One of them, which was getting a particularly hot time from enemy ack-ack, had a bullet in his ammunition box. This blew up a number of cartridges, as a result of which the Mustang was simply riddled with splinters.

"The wing was damaged and the pilot wounded, but he got the aircraft home and landed it safely."

Tactical reports from Royal Air Force Army Co-operation units were laudatory such as this given by W/Cdr. Peter Dudjeon, former squadron commander of one of these units, concerning Mustang Mark Is and IAs.

"The long range of this aircraft made it an excellent tactical reconnaissance aircraft and its armament made it effective against most ground targets. As their operations progressed, they swung more and more to offensive reconnaissance and began to take advantage of targets of opportunity until the operation finally developed into a strategic effort against ground objectives such as railway locomotives, canal barges, heavy motor transport and aircraft on the ground.

"These daylight intrusion raids (rhubarbs) were very successful, largely due to the care and effort which went into the planning and operations of their missions. The theme was the destruction of those targets designated with the minimum number of casualties. That this was achieved is attested by the record of this squadron which in eighteen months of operations destroyed or damaged severely, 200 locomotives, over 200 barges and an undetermined number of enemy aircraft on the ground. This was accomplished with only one Mustang being shot down by enemy fighters, five planes lost to enemy flak and two vanished without record as to their fate. During this period of operations, they were never once intercepted over enemy territory. This included raids over Holland, occupied France, Belgium and Germany, the longest one having been a flight over 1000 miles. Their furthermost victory was a locomotive shot up just outside Wilhelmshaven, an airline distance of approximately 350 miles from their base.

"It has been found that the Mustang is faster than the Me 109 and the FW 190 and that 4000 to 8000 feet is a good altitude at which to catch the enemy. At sea level, the Mustang can run away from any enemy aircraft they have encountered to date. The pilots are schooled to run rather than fight because their main object is the destruction of ground targets, not to fight enemy aircraft. They are instructed in the use of flaps in combat to reduce their turning radius. At least one FW 190 has been made to spin in through the use of a small amount of flap by the Mustang then engaged in a turning contest at low altitude. The 190 tried to tighten his turn to keep the Mustang in his sights after the pilot had dropped his flaps slightly, but spun out of the turn."

One Mustang pilot who decided to mix it up a bit was P/O R. P. Bethell of No. 268 Squadron flying with a four-plane patrol off Snailwell on the afternoon of November 26, 1942. Bethell saw an Me 109F at 1500 feet so he climbed to the attack and fired a four-second burst at 250 yards, seeing strikes. He closed and fired another burst at 200 yards, rapidly closing to point-blank range. The 109 burst into flames and crashed. Shortly after this encounter he saw a Junkers Ju 52 transport lumbering along the coast at 500 feet. Attacking immediately, he let fly with a long burst and

An excellent view of the Mustang IA. This Allison-powered craft had carburetor intake on top of cowling. (RCAF)

continued to fire while closing the gap from 300 to 50 yards. The Junkers poured heavy smoke, crashed and exploded.

Pilots of the Royal Canadian Air Force inaugurated night intruder missions with Mustangs in the spring of 1943. On the night of April 13, P/O Peters and F/O F. M. "Bitsy" Grant took off and set course for the darkened skies of France to seek their prey. This evening, luck would be with them. In the Paris area, Grant found night-flying training taking place. Stealthfully he closed in on the tail of a Dornier 217, gave him a short squirt of lead and saw him crash in a ball of fire. With all guns of the installation now alerted, the two pilots went "balls out" for home.

F/O F. E. Hanton had one of the Canadians' better nights intruding in a Mustang. Roaring over the French countryside, Hanton spotted a train in motion near Vire and dived on it with all guns blazing. The locomotive absorbed a lethal dose of lead, and clouds of steam rose in the summer darkness as the train came to an abrupt halt.

Continuing on to the Rennes airdrome, the Mustang pilot sighted several enemy aircraft in the landing pattern of the lit-up field. Just what he had been waiting for! Immediately he lined up a Junkers Ju 88 and gave it a good burst. The German pilot instantly cut his navigation lights and went into a dive. The brilliant flash of his guns served as just enough of a blinder to make Hanton lose his target.

Continuing his nocturnal quest, Hanton next sighted a Messerschmitt 110 on his final approach. Diving down, the Canadian gave the Luftwaffe craft a short burst and watched it dive right on into the ground. As he pulled up over his victim, Hanton found himself in the middle of intense flak and probing searchlight fingers. Diving for the deck, he headed for home.

Mustang Is and IAs saw combat with the Royal Air Force up until 1944, and as the records attest, performed magnificently. The days of conquest over the Luftwaffe at high altitude came later with the Merlin-powered models, but as a low-altitude, interdiction and reconnaissance aircraft, the early Mustang knew few equals. Truly, the pony from North American had won its spurs.

CHAPTER **2**

THE INVADER

IN THE spring of 1942 a new version of the P-51A was evolved specifically for dive bombing. This craft was fitted with wing-mounted air brakes, a 1325 h.p. Allison V-1710-87 engine and was designated the A-36A. Five hundred A-36s were built for the AAF, but the majority of its combat was centered around two fighter-bomber groups in the Mediterranean Theater of Operations—the 27th and the 86th.

Both of these units arrived in North Africa in the late spring of 1943, just after the close of the Tunisian campaign, and saw their first action during the reduction by air of the island of Pantelleria. The men of the A-36s had been told in the United States that their dive brakes would be all but useless and the best thing to do was to wire them closed. This proved to be a very incorrect appraisal and they were used throughout the Sicilian campaign and the Italian invasion with great success.

A-36A, in natural finish, during preflight. (MENARD)

An A-36A in olive-drab war paint. The Invader proved to be an excellent dive bomber and strafing aircraft. (USAF)

Not only was the A-36 a fine dive-bombing aircraft, it proved to be a very stable and effective ground strafer. The quietness of its engine enabled it to get right on top of ground targets before the enemy realized it was in the vicinity, and the scream of the dive flaps gained the A-36 the name of "screaming helldivers" by the Germans.

The A-36 was known to American forces as the Invader and it really lived up to its name, for it was to see yeoman service during both the invasion of Sicily and of Italy. It was during the Sicilian campaign that the airplane proved itself and gained the everlasting praise of the pilots that flew it.

Dive bombing was usually carried out from an altitude of approximately 10,000 to 12,000 feet. The A-36 would break out into single file and make their dive-bombing runs in single file. Bombing speed would be held to around 290–300 miles per hour when the dive brakes were extended full. Bombs were dropped about 3000 feet and pullout was accomplished at approximately 1500 feet. Bombing was very accurate and it wasn't unusual for hits to stack up right on top of the target.

The A-36 carried six .50-caliber machine guns, two firing through the propeller and two in each wing. For their primary mission of ground strafing, the Invader pilots usually had their guns synchronized to concentrate their fire at 200–250 yards. The impact of such a force was enough to bring about the destruction of almost anything they encountered on the ground.

As a ground strafer, the A-36 could take it and still come home. One lieutenant was returning from a mission on the west coast of Italy when he sighted a staff car traveling along at high speed. He made a sharp turn to go down and at such a steep angle that it was difficult to judge the terrain. As he concentrated on his target, he got a little low and went between two trees.

The left aileron was torn completely off, along with two and a half feet of the left wing. The right wing, from the pitot tube outboard, was slashed back halfway through the wing section, but did not break off.

The pilot started a gradual climb and circle to gain altitude in an attempt to bring the plane back to home base. He then pulled the emergency canopy release and had to bump the canopy off as he was still in a climb. The plane had to be steered by tail alone, but was operating satisfactorily. There was a short burst from the right machine guns, probably due to a short in the wiring, so the pilot cut the gun switch and continued climbing.

Fire broke out in the gun section of the right wing and the ammunition started firing, so he figured it was time to depart. The pilot bailed out.

Many strange and some amusing things occurred during the Sicilian campaign. The pilots were always out after locomotives when they could locate them. On one occasion the Italian engineer was most co-operative. The A-36s flew a course parallel to the train and the engineer sighted them and brought his train to an immediate halt. Waving to the pilots, he jumped from the cab and ran for cover. The fighter-bombers then proceeded to shoot up the train.

Many Sicilians would assist the pilots by pointing out camouflaged targets on the ground. The A-36s would come over low and the peasants would wave and point to German installations hidden in the trees.

Lt. Robert E. Fromm sighted a convoy of German light tanks on one of his missions. He opened fire and saw his tracers strike a tank and then he lined up on his second target, a truck.

"Thirty feet off the ground and nose slightly down, I sent six streams of lead into the truck. Instantly there was an explosion which enveloped him in flames and dark smoke. I had shot up an ammunition carrier.

North American A-36 of the Twelfth Air Force flies over Mt. Vesuvius, Italy. The Invaders flew much of the air cover over Anzio beachhead. (USAF)

"That was my first bad break. The second came a moment later when my plane which was partially damaged by the blast came out of the smoke at better than 400 miles per hour and plowed into a tree.

"I should say plowed through a tree. The plane continued to fly, but I knew it couldn't stay up for long. I climbed to 500 feet and I rose in my cockpit to bail out. But I looked down and saw Germans. I decided to stay with my ship for a while, as long as it would stay with me."

The plane did stay with Fromm, although he could get it no faster than 160 nor higher than 900 feet.

With wings badly damaged, fuselage torn and dented, engine streaming smoke, his machine guns camouflaged by tree branches, he flew back toward friendly territory.

Fromm thought he had it made, but found himself over a flak area. "I couldn't take evasive action, so I flew straight through it."

He came down to land, thinking he had two wheels, but he had only one. "I knew I landed on one wheel. So I lowered the left wing a bit. The field was slippery and when the left wing hit the runway it skidded along instead of catching." Fromm stepped out uninjured.

Lt. J. B. Walton, of the 27th Group, had this to say of a typical day's strafing, "We started after a convoy of fifty to seventy-five trucks. The captain went after the trucks ahead and I took those on the right. One truck started to turn back off the road and got caught in a gully and I got him just as he toppled over.

"Then I swung over to the side of the mountain we were passing. There were two trucks carrying about thirty men each. The men started running and I got both trucks. Then I went over a hill and got three more—all big trucks hauling men. Got them clean; I could see my tracers kicking up the dust around them. Then our flight ran into a locomotive and I saw it go up in steam. There was some ack-ack around this and I could see men standing around a gun. I was over to the right and they didn't see me. I shot all the men on the gun and damaged the gun."

Walton tells of another day when American armored columns were trying to get around a narrow strip of sandy beach. "Each time one of our tanks would stick his nose around the bend, a hidden 88-mm gun would open up. The tankers called for air support and the A-36s came in to see what we could do about the situation. The tank commander said he would risk one more tank and for us to see if we could spot the culprit. Just as the tank showed itself, the Germans fired a round and we spotted the gun. It was on a mountainside inside a farm house. We then proceeded to remove the nuisance."

Lt. Wendell Hook of the 86th Group had always wondered if self-sealing tanks were as effective as the manufacturers claimed. He found out one day when he was pulling up from a target in string formation. A 20-mm shell had gone through the left wing tank of the A-36 that he was trailing. For a few seconds, gas leaked out rapidly. Then it stopped. The pilot continued back to base some 100 or so miles away and landed. Hook had found out what he wanted to know.

Another A-36 pilot came in on a target over Italy, flying only forty feet above the ground. He gave it a short burst at 300 yards and a violent explosion occurred. As he was almost over the target he had to fly right into the erupting debris. Exploding shells came through the floor of the cockpit, but luckily he was not wounded. The wings were full of holes and the ailerons were almost blown off. Large holes up to six inches in diameter were blown in the wings and the metal was peeled up and jagged.

There were holes in every section of the wings and the right wing tip was partly torn loose and pointing upward. The horizontal stabilizers were bent upward and full of holes and the leading edge of the left horizontal stabilizer was blown away. The rudder and elevators were still controllable. The cockpit was filled with smoke, but the pilot noted that he had 1200 feet of altitude.

After flying some twenty miles, the engine started to quit, so the pilot bailed out. He was picked up shortly by an Italian speedboat and was made prisoner. A few days later he was turned over to the Americans when they captured the small island where he was being held.

On another mission several of the Invaders of the 27th Group were flying at minimum altitude. They were just above the whitecaps off the coast of Italy when the geysers of water began to kick up beneath them. At first the pilots paid little attention to them and one even stated that he thought they were porpoises playing. Then it was discovered that the planes were being fired upon by 88-mm guns on the coast! Suddenly an 88-mm burst sent a column of water up right in front of one of the A-36s. The pilot didn't have time to recover; his plane hit the water with a smack but stayed right side up. The pilot, uninjured, went over the side, got into his dinghy and paddled to shore. He, too, was liberated in a short time when Italy was invaded.

The A-36s didn't see too much aerial combat, but their pilots had always been told that they were no match for the Me 109 at high altitude. If bounced by Germans, they were to salvo their bombs and force the fight to their altitude below 8000 feet; preferably below 5000.

These tactics paid off for three A-36 pilots who encountered enemy opposition south of Rome. The Americans, a flight of eight, had been flying along at about 300 mph, shooting up ground targets and flying so close to the ground that they had to pull up to get over the trees when they spotted a flight of three Me 109s.

Lt. Eugene Santala related, "The Me's were also low, but higher enough for us that they didn't see us, although they were only about a quarter of a mile away. We turned and chased them for five minutes, keeping low. Just as they banked to come into their field to land, they saw us. But it was too late then, for we already closed up.

"I picked up my target, having advantage since I was leading the flight. The Me seemed to fall apart. The wreckage fell practically on the field. F/O James F. Roberts, who was flying my wing and had shot a short burst at a plane, slipped down to the air base and perforated an He 111— it blew up."

Lt. Robert V. Allen then cut off the second Me 109 and shot it down. The third German, in a desperate attempt to avoid the A-36s, cut away and headed for the nearby mountain with the Americans in hot pursuit. Five times the planes roared around the peak. Then the leading Invader lost his pole position among the A-36s when he skidded off course in the attempt to close for a shot. He tried to fly over the mountain and get at Jerry from an angle, but this failed, too. The second pilot hung close to the Messerschmitt's tail, managed to gain a little and finally filled his sights with the 109. A short burst was all that it took.

The most successful A-36 pilot, as far as enemy aircraft went, was Lt. Michael T. Russo. He had his biggest day on December 30, 1943, when he led a twelve-plane formation to attack a railroad station near Rome. While flying at 14,000 feet approaching the target, sixteen Me 109s attacked the A-36s. Remembering his teachings, Russo immediately took his flight down to 8000 feet with the enemy in hot pursuit. At this altitude the A-36 could give the Messerschmitts trouble and this they did. Turning into the enemy, the Invaders broke up the formation and Russo accounted for two of the fighters before the dogfight ended.

The A-36 which had shown excellence in bombing, strafing and as a low-altitude fighter, even demonstrated further diversification when it was used as a supply craft. After Salerno, Lt. Walton, his C.O. and two other pilots flew food and ammunition in to some stranded American paratroops. The packages were heavily wrapped and hung on the bomb racks of the Invaders to such an extent that they could hardly get off the ground. All the way to the drop zone the pilots had to fight to maintain control as the bulky packages tried to sway in the racks. Finally they made the drop zone and let the bundles go at zero altitude. The supplies were delivered in good shape.

Maintenance on the A-36s proved to be excellent. No great difficulties were experienced and the majority of the aircraft were kept flyable. The ground crews of the 86th got a rare chance to appreciate the results of their good work when the group moved to Italy in mid-September of 1943.

The unit had just moved to Sele strip when they were called upon to destroy a large tobacco-factory building on the outskirts of Battipaglia. The factory buildings were serving as stronghold for some twelve 88-mm guns and 150-plus Germans that were holding up the advance of the X Corps.

At one o'clock on the afternoon of September 17, the first squadron of the 86th took off and swung out over the bay to get altitude. Then they came back across the field and made a turn to the south along the main coast road. That brought them over the target. Down they went, raining their 500-pound packages of destruction. At Sele strip the ground crews stood and watched the bombs which they had loaded only fifteen minutes previously fall on the factory.

A second attack was made on the German stronghold late that afternoon and a third early the next morning. Shortly after the last raid the X Corps moved forward and took over. The 86th had blown the place to bits. Twelve guns and over a hundred Germans were found in the wreckage.

A quarter of a century later, much is still written and spoken regarding the immortal P-51 Mustang, but little is remembered of her sister, the A-36 Invader. Yet they did a tremendous job in those days of 1943 when so much hung in the balance. When our ground troops needed air support so badly, it was the A-36s that gave it to them. Surely these infantrymen have never forgotten this aircraft, nor have the surviving Germans who still recall the screaming demon of the Mediterranean.

CHAPTER 3

AAF MUSTANGS IN ENGLAND

I N T H E late summer and early fall of 1943, the bombers of the Eighth Air Force had suffered heavy casualties at the hands of the Luftwaffe fighters. The primary cause of these losses was the inability of their escort to accompany them all the way to such targets as Schweinfurt and Regensburg, deep in Germany. The utilization of two 108-gallon drop tanks provided the P-47s with a theoretical range of only 375 miles at the very most, and this didn't allow for aerial encounters. A few Lockheed P-38s were in England, but their range wouldn't allow them to go all the way with the bombers, either. The operational planners wanted desperately to begin an all-out bombing campaign against the industries underlying the Luftwaffe, but with no long-range escort fighters, further deep penetration into Germany by the Eighth Air Force bombers was out of the question.

A few early P-51As and F-6s had found their way into the tactical-reconnaissance units of the Eighth Air Force at this time, but the first of the Mustangs destined for the fighter units had not arrived. Operational leaders in England were well aware of the extended range of the P-51 and were anxious to give it a test as bomber escort, even though the Mustang would not be able to go to all targets with the bombers until it was fitted with drop tanks. Regardless, the arrival of the new craft was eagerly awaited in the theater. Suprisingly, the first fighter unit to be equipped with the Mustang in England would be assigned not to the Eighth Air Force, but to the Ninth!

On November 4, 1943, a tired but eager group of young pilots was unceremoniously delivered to the airdrome at Greenham Commons in England. New to the European Theater and with no combat experience, they were still awed with the whole situation and, other than rumor, had no idea that they were to pioneer a new concept in fighter-escort tactics. They were

A shiny new P-51B displays its clean lines and greenhouse-type canopy.
(MCDOWELL)

the 354th Fighter Group and it was their good fortune to have been selected to become the first P-51 Mustang fighter unit in England.

Jubilation was the order of the day for Lt. Col. Kenneth R. Martin's Ninth Air Force pilots at Greenham Commons when orders came down for him to select a nucleus of pilots to train on the P-51As of the 67th Tactical Reconnaissance Group. After a few days of flying, these pilots returned to Boxted where their own Mustangs had begun to arrive. The newcomers immediately fell in love with the craft and the 354th adopted the name of the "Pioneer Mustang" Group.

The Eighth Air Force had watched the training and performance of the 354th with anxious eyes, and as the group neared the time of its initial operation, it found itself still the property of the Ninth Air Force, but assigned to the Eighth Air Force for operations.

By December 1, 1943, the unit had received fifty-four P-51Bs and three P-51B-5s, and on this date twenty-four planes and pilots were dispatched on a familiarization sweep over the Knocke-St. Omer-Calais area. This sweep was led by the famed leader of the 4th Fighter Group, Col. Don Blakeslee, a former RCAF and Eagle Squadron pilot. The steely-eyed Blakeslee greatly impressed the new Mustang pilots in briefing that morning when he informed them that in a head-on attack from the enemy, his pilots didn't break. When a young pilot asked him, "What if the German doesn't break either?" his reply was, "Son, you will have earned your hazardous duty pay."

The 354th encountered their first enemy aircraft on December 13 while escorting the bombers to Kiel. Lt. Glenn T. Eagleston along with Lt. Wallace Emmer were in a two-plane formation when they observed an Me 110 about 3000 feet below them. Eagleston peeled off under Lt. Emmer and came in on the tail of the Messerschmitt. His first burst of gunfire seemed to have no effect, but on his second pass the P-51 pilot silenced the rear gunner.

"As I came in again I fired short bursts from 300 yards astern and from slightly above. I knocked out the 110's right engine which burst into flame, parts flying off the engine. I broke off at extremely close range. On my fourth pass I came in from astern and slightly above, but my guns were jammed and I broke off without firing," reported Eagleston.

The Me 110 was last observed in a shallow dive with the right engine out and aflame, heading down into the overcast. A Mustang pilot had made the first of many marks against the Luftwaffe even if the claim did have to go down in the records as a probable.

The first confirmed victory of an AAF Mustang pilot was gained by Lt. Charles F. Gumm of the 354th while escorting B-17s to Bremen on December 16. In his own words, "While climbing in mutual support position with Lieutenant Talbot toward the lead box of bombers, we sighted four Me 109s starting to queue up behind the second box of bombers. We climbed after them, and when in about 400-yards range, two enemy aircraft saw us and broke left and straight down. We closed on the other two and I dropped back a little to cover Lieutenant Talbot's tail, but his 109 saw him and broke left and down.

"I was then almost in position to fire on mine who was still flying straight for the bombers. Lieutenant Talbot pulled up and to the right to cover my tail while I closed to about 100 yards. I fired a two-second burst, noticing no effects. Closed to about 60 yards and fired a three-second burst, noticing a thin trail of smoke coming from the right side of the engine. I fired again at very close range and was showered with smoke, oil and pieces which I pulled up through, and glanced back to see him going down to the left with a large roll of smoke coming from the right side of the engine. Then I looked for Lieutenant Talbot again and saw him chasing a 109 and another 109 closing in on him. Went down after the last 109 and they broke straight down and we went back to the bombers."

The Pioneer Mustangs had their first big day on January 5, 1944, when Maj. Jim Howard led them to Kiel to give the "big friends" target and

Col. Jim Howard's "Ding Hao!" so named in remembrance of his days in China with the "Flying Tigers." (TURNER)

withdrawal escort. In the area between Meldorf and Kiel, large concentrations of twin-engine fighters were encountered. Scores of Me 110s were lobbing their rockets into the bomber formations when the Mustangs tore into them and completely routed their attacks. When Jim Howard rounded up his P-51s to come home, eighteen of the enemy had been shot from the sky while Lt. Warren Emerson, who had been hit by 20-mm fragments, was the only casualty of the 354th.

Six days later, Major Howard led the group again; this time to Halberstadt and Oschersleben. The fighters were assigned to provide target support for the bombers, and upon rendezvous he positioned his Mustangs up and down over the bombers. In adherence with normal escort tactics, the P-51s broke up into flights of four and positioned themselves above and to the sides of their assigned bomber units. From this vantage point they enjoyed freedom of movement over the Fortresses, yet they held an altitude advantage over any German fighters that might rise to intercept the bombers.

The first enemy opposition was encountered as the bombers passed over the target. Mustangs dived down in an attempt to head them off, and in the melee, the eager pilots jumped the gun and cut in front of Major Howard, causing him to have to pull out of the attack. Alone, he headed for another bomber formation that was under attack and the events that then transpired are best related by Jim Howard.

"When I regained bomber altitude, I discovered I was alone and in the vicinity of the forward boxes of bombers. There was one box of B-17s in particular that seemed to be under attack by six single- and twin-engined enemy fighters. There were about twenty bombers in a very compact formation and the fighters were working individually.

"The first plane I got was a two-engined German night fighter. I went down after him, gave him several squirts and watched him crash. He stood out very clearly, silhouetted against the snow that covered the ground. He went down in a cloud of black smoke and fire and hit the ground.

"Shortly after that, a Focke-Wulf came cruising along beneath me. He pulled up into the sun when he saw me. I gave him a squirt and I almost ran into his canopy when he threw it off to get out. He bailed out.

"Then I circled trying to join up with the other P-51s. I saw an Me 109 just underneath and a few hundred yards ahead of me. He saw me at the same time and chopped his throttle, hoping my speed would carry me ahead of him. It's an old trick. He started scissoring underneath me, but I chopped my throttle and started scissoring at the same time and then we went into a circle dogfight, and it was a matter of who could maneuver best and cut the shortest circle.

"I dumped 20-degree flaps and began cutting inside of him, so he quit and went into a dive with me after him. I got on his tail and got in some long-distance squirts from 300 or 400 yards. I got some strikes on him but didn't see him hit the ground.

"I pulled up again and saw an Me 109 and a P-51 running along together. The Mustang saw me coming in from behind and he peeled off while the Messerschmitt started a slow circle. I don't remember whether I shot at him or not. Things happen so fast it's hard to remember things in sequence when you get back."

However, the bomber crewmen remembered. On his return, the commander of the B-17 group immediately got on the telephone to Eighth Air Force Headquarters to report the show that had been put on by a Mustang pilot who had taken on some thirty German fighters alone and had shot down six of them! Howard was identified through the "buzz number" on his airplane and the military and the press descended upon him. Initially, all the information that they could get out of the modest Howard was, "I seen my duty and I done it."

Jim Howard's combat report doesn't mention the other enemy aircraft that he fired upon that were seen to go down by the men of the B-17s, nor would he even claim more than three. Regardless of his reticence, his

*Col. Jim Howard of the 354th Fighter Group, Ninth Air Force, receives
the Congressional Medal of Honor from Gen. Carl A. Spaatz for his action
of January 11, 1944.* (USAF)

extraordinary feat and heroism were recognized with the award of the
Congressional Medal of Honor.

Other Mustang pilots of the 354th downed another dozen German
fighters that day for the loss of none of their own.

While victory was steadily increasing for the Mustangs, there had
been hardship, too. Not only were pilots being lost to some of the better
members of the Luftwaffe, but the P-51s ran into increasing difficulties
from their fellow escort pilots. This stemmed from a recognition problem.
The P-51 at a quick glance bore a close resemblance to the German
Messerschmitt 109. More than once the Mustangs were attacked by P-47s,
and there were occasions when they were damaged so badly that they
barely managed to limp home. Lt. Glenn Eagleston, who was destined to
become the top-scoring ace of the Ninth Air Force, was one of these victims.
He was shot up so badly on one mission that he was forced to bail out over

England. Some vehement letters from the 354th to Headquarters of the Eighth Fighter Command brought about some intensive aircraft recognition classes for the Thunderbolt pilots in England.

It wasn't all friendly opposition that was proving costly to the Mustangs, however, and at times the P-51 really had to show its stuff to get home to England. One of these early mission incidents is related by Lt. Clayton Gross.

"We had escorted a bomber group to Frankfurt on February 8, 1944, without a sign of the Luftwaffe, and reluctantly turned for home at the end of our tour without a man breaking the tapes on his guns. In the process of escorting the big friends we had separated into elements, and by chance when we started home, Lieutenant Radojits and I joined with an element led by Lt. Jim Daglish.

"After maybe thirty minutes we spotted a lone Messerschmitt 109 at about 2000 feet, silhouetted against a solid overcast. Naturally, Daglish and I had a race to get to him, but he popped into the overcast. We were quite disappointed and began to climb again; still watching the place for his exit. We were up a few thousand feet when he reappeared. Again we went down, but lost him again. As we began to climb again in mutual support, we still focused some attention on the cloud cover, although we had no intention of going down again. I casually glanced over to Daglish's element on my left and was astonished to see four FW 190s boring in on his tail.

"I screamed for them to break left so that Tony Radojits and I might fall in behind the attackers. Jim's wingman was hit severely as they began to break. (He was downed.) I screamed again for Tony to follow me and broke hard left to get in behind the Focke-Wulfs as they went after Jim. When Tony didn't answer, I stole a quick glance over my shoulder and lo and behold, Tony was gone, and I had four Focke-Wulfs on my own tail and already firing at me. I recall that I wished Daglish the best of luck and continued my roll left to the inverted position, at which time I pulled back and headed for that friendly cloud cover at 2000 feet.

"I entered the undercast at some ungodly speed with no instrument uncaged and no idea of what lay below me. I can recall how great the landscape looked below when I pulled out without hitting anything. I had placed the throttle through the gate into "war emergency" (i.e., an extreme throttle setting which allowed absolute full-engine power. Normally, five minutes operation at this setting was enough to damage vital engine parts.) as soon as I leveled off, because I expected the entire Luftwaffe to be behind me at any moment. I went to the deck—and I mean grass cutting—and immediately set sail for home.

Capt. Clayton K. Gross and "Live Bait." Gross learned that the Mustang can absorb a lot of punishment and still come home. (GROSS)

"The first item which popped in front of me as I steered for England was a locomotive which required no movement on my part to hit as I approached. I remember my feelings as I passed over it. I knew I was going down and I thought, 'Oh, boy, that's going to make them mad.'

"A few minutes later I saw a truck on the highway at about my level, and since it had German markings, I proceeded to blast it, after which I again experienced some regrets thinking about the consequences as soon as they got me.

"I had several targets which I could not resist and I think the same thoughts entered my mind each time. I truthfully did not relax until I reached the English Channel, and then not very much. Incidentally, at one time from my 1½-foot level, I spotted heavy power lines in front of me and for some reason reefed back in an attempt to clear them. I didn't make it. There was a tremendous explosion as I flew through them, but it stayed in the air. When I landed, I discovered that the collision with the wires had cracked my windshield, torn the air scoop off leaving the radiator exposed, imbedded a 2½-foot length of copper cable in the radiator and had taken a part of the wing tip off.

"This incident plus the fact that as I circled to land I discovered that I was still in war emergency and had been for a period of forty-five minutes or over, instead of the maximum five minutes, was nothing short of a miracle."

Neither Gross nor Daglish's wingmen returned from the mission.

The P-51B with its 70-gallon fuselage and internal wing tanks could escort to a point approximately 475 miles from base, a distance which was 100 miles better than the maximum escort range of the P-47 equipped with two 108-gallon wing tanks. Early in March of 1944 the Mustang demonstrated what it could do with two 75-gallon wing tanks as it increased its range to 650 miles from base. Later, with two 108-gallon tanks, it illustrated its versatility by increasing escort range to 850 miles. The bombers then had an escort that could go anywhere they could go. The time had come to penetrate all the way into the very heart of the Third Reich; the target— Berlin!

There were four P-51 groups operational in England at this time. The Pioneer Mustang 354th, the 357th Group which entered combat with the Eighth Air Force on February 10, 1944, the 363rd Group of the Ninth Air Force which was also assigned to the Eighth for operations. Through persistence, Col. Don Blakeslee obtained the sleek Rolls-Royce-powered craft for his 4th Fighter Group of the Eighth Air Force on February 25, 1944.

The bombers and their escorts were briefed to strike the Berlin area on March 3, 1944, but when airborne that day, the weather proved to be appalling. All aircraft were instructed to abort the mission, but the call didn't get through to all of them. Nine pilots of the 4th Fighter Group searching for their big friends between Berlin and Hamburg found themselves surrounded by some sixty to eighty enemy aircraft.

Led by Capt. Don Gentile, the Mustang pilots dropped their tanks and turned into the attack. Two pair of FW 190s split-essed and immediately two P-51s raced after them. This was just what the Germans wanted, for immediately Luftwaffe fighters pounced on the pursuing P-51s and shot one of the Americans from the sky.

Desperately, Gentile fought his way out of the encircling trap and then blazed back into the melee to help out. Quickly he lined up on an Me 110, only to have his canopy frost up. Reefing in tightly, he fired a burst at a twin-engined Dornier 217 and registered good strikes before his gunsight went out.

Breaking off combat, he went streaking across to assist Lt. W. W. Millikan who was in difficulty, but at the same instant, Gentile came under successive head-on attacks from four, two and then eight 190s. Slamming his throttle to the fire wall, Don climbed sunward as his supercharger cut in. A 190 loomed ahead. He gave him a squirt using Kentucky windage to compensate for his inoperative gunsight. The Focke-Wulf flamed.

Lt. Vermont Garrison blasted one enemy aircraft, and then with only one gun firing, he picked off another with a deflection shot.

Lt. K. E. "Swede" Carlson and three others went after a number of Me 110s that had gone into a protective lufbery circle. "Swede" decided his tail-on approach wasn't going to work so he reversed his tactics and went after them in the opposite direction. One of the Messerschmitts broke out to attack. Carlson fired and hit the Me 110's port engine and the German went down.

Eight of the Luftwaffe fighters had fallen to the Mustangs when the Debden-based boys tore away to make their run for home. However, the ordeal of the remaining P-51s wasn't over. Increasing bad weather and squalls forced them to the deck. The flak batteries were by this time fully alerted and multicolored balls of fire began to arc the sky.

As four of the P-51s raced over a town, fireworks erupted with a vengeance. Lt. Vermont Garrison took a hit, bade his mates farewell, jettisoned his canopy and bailed out. For the quiet ace from Kentucky, the war was over.

Capt. Don Gentile of the 4th Fighter Group stands on the wing of his P-51B "Shangri-La." (USAF)

An FW 190 takes hits on the fuselage from the P-51 that was right on his tail. (RUST)

Lieutenant Millikan managed to limp into Manston in England with five gallons of fuel left in his tanks. An utterly exhausted pilot pulled himself from the cockpit, shakily descended from the wing, dropped to his knees and pounded the ground. After six hours of strife his Mustang had brought him home. Seven of the nine P-51s had made their way back.

On March 4, the bombers went back to the Berlin area in spite of a continuation of foul weather. Leading the pack was Col. Don Blakeslee and his red-nosed 4th Fighter Group. This day the pilots would taste blood once more, and better yet, they actually got to see Berlin through breaks in the clouds before encountering the enemy. However, Blakeslee knew utter frustration when he pulled in on the tail of an Me 109 and his guns refused to fire. Grimly, he pushed his throttle forward and pulled alongside the 109 whose pilot answered his signal of disgust with a cheery wave. His only claim to fame that day had been that he was the first Mustang pilot over Berlin.

Herein lay one of the few difficulties that was experienced on the P-51B Mustang. Gun stoppages became quite annoying for a period of time until the cause was discovered and remedied. Due to the thin profile of the wing, the guns mounted there had been canted to the inboard rather than mounted upright. In the course of combat maneuvers, "g" forces tended to cause the ammunition belts to bind, causing jamming. Installation of ammo-booster motors rectified this situation in short order.

Fifty-caliber slugs strike home on Messerschmitt 109 as Mustang closes for the kill. (RUST)

Another unit was to taste defeat at the hands of the Luftwaffe the morning of the fourth of March. Forty-eight P-51s of the 363rd Fighter Group set out from Rivenhall airfield as target escort to the big friends to the Hamburg area. Heavy clouds were encountered and the formation became scattered and off course. Near the target, the flights of two squadrons were bounced by Me 109s of II/JG 1 who claimed to have destroyed twelve of the Mustangs for the loss of only one of their own. This tragic loss was the worst that the P-51 groups in the ETO would ever experience.

On March 6, 1944, the whole Eighth Air Force went to Berlin and, seemingly, the entire Luftwaffe came up to do battle. The 354th Group encountered over fifty of the enemy just after rendezvous, but these didn't want to mix it up. In the Brandenberg area a number of twin-engined, rocket-laden craft were engaged, and then some 109s got in on the act. The Pioneer Mustangs claimed nine that day for the loss of one P-51.

The 357th Group which had only entered combat in February had one of their best days. Twenty Luftwaffe aircraft fell before their guns for no losses. The 4th Group did almost as well in downing seventeen. Maj. Howard "Deacon" Hively had nailed one Me 109, and got some good strikes on another when the German nosed over and dived straight down. Hively tucked his plane right behind the Messerschmitt and followed him until the

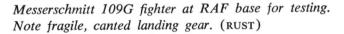

Messerschmitt 109G fighter at RAF base for testing.
Note fragile, canted landing gear. (RUST)

An excellent view of "Killer," a P-51B with Malcolm hood, as flown by Maj. Bob Stephens of the 354th Fighter Group. (USAF)

Me 109 hit the ground. His admiration for his Mustang is appropriately expressed in his combat report:

"A Mustang can outturn, outclimb, outdive and outrun Messerschmitt 109s."

Lt. Johnny Godfrey also put a 109 in the trees that day. After three head-on passes, the Mustang pilot maneuvered in behind the Messerschmitt and chased him right down on the deck among the trees. Abruptly, Godfrey snapped the stick back into his gut, but the German didn't make it. One

Last moments of a Messerschmitt 110 as a Mustang closes rapidly on its tail.
(RUST)

wing was sheared off by the trees and the balance went cart-wheeling through
the foliage.

The 354th Group received unexpected good news from a German
broadcast on April 7. Their commander, Col. Kenneth Martin, had been
lost on a mission to Frankfurt on February 11 when he collided with a
German fighter. His pilots had last seen him spinning earthwards after the
collision.

The German announcer related, "I have just returned from a visit to a
hospital where I went to see an old friend of mine, who is a fighter pilot.
I found my friend sitting up in bed, all smiles. He told me that he had been
ordered to attack when U.S. bombers were over this country. He was approaching the enemy when suddenly he saw an enemy fighter coming straight
for him at a distance of about a mile. He was piloting an Me 109 and the
enemy plane was a Mustang. He did not swerve from his course; both
machines were blazing away with their guns as they approached one another.
They met full blast head-on. The German pilot remembers unbuckling his
strap, then he found himself in the air, pulled his rip cord and came to earth
with no more than a broken arm.

"I went to see Colonel Martin, who was in bed. He had the plaster
cast taken off his left lower arm that morning and was then exercising his
fingers which had grown stiff. His only other injury was a broken right leg,
still in plaster."

Spring of 1944 saw the 352nd, 355th, 359th and 361st Fighter Groups
of the Eighth Air Force trading their P-47s for Mustangs. Also entering
combat with the P-51 was the 339th Fighter Group which had just arrived
in the theater. The versatile ponies had shown their hooves to the Luftwaffe
and were now ranging all over Germany with the bombers. Desperately,

the hard-pressed German pilots took to the skies, but the P-51s were always there and in ever-increasing numbers.

A little over a month after the 352nd Group traded its P-47s for blue-nosed Mustangs, one of its pilots became the first in the ETO to blast five enemy aircraft out of the air on one mission. The group as a whole had a terrific day with twenty-seven planes destroyed, which was outstanding enough to warrant a Presidential Unit Citation in their first big battle with the new airplanes.

The fighters had just rendezvoused with the bombers just short of Brunswick when gaggles of 109s and 190s arrived on the scene. Over a hundred were flying in groups of fifteen to twenty, and all noses were determinedly pointed at the bombers.

The Mustangs proceeded to break up into elements and attack the enemy force. Lt. Carl Luksic picked out a batch of fighters and chased them down to 3000 feet where he lost them. With only his wingman, Lieutenant O'Nan, he leveled out and heard O'Nan sing out over the R/T, "There's a 109 ahead."

Luksic couldn't spot him so he told O'Nan to take care of him while he covered him. "During the chase, I saw six 190s coming in from my left headed for the bombers, so I immediately turned into the sextette.

"I fired very short bursts from about 300 yards on the nearest 190, the tail-end Charlie. I saw many strikes on the canopy and fuselage. The pilot stopped short, rolled his ship over and bailed out. A moment later I saw the pilot of the plane that Lieutenant O'Nan hit bail out, too.

"The leader of these 190s evidently saw what had happened. He whipped his formation around and one of them started shooting at me. It became a rat race, with all of us going around in circles. Somewhere in this merry-go-round I managed to get on the tail of one of them. I fired a couple of bursts—but I'm sure none of them went home. The German must have gotten scared, for the next thing I knew he went into a spin. I saw him crash and explode.

"I shopped around for a while, thinking I could find some more targets to shoot at. I saw a lone plane at a distance, which I couldn't quite make out. It might have been friendly, but I wasn't sure, so I went to investigate. When I was 25 yards back of it I realized it was a bandit. I fired once. Next thing I knew I was flying his wing, right beside him. My speed had brought me right up to him. He looked at me. I looked back. I must have scared the hell out of him, for the next thing I knew he jettisoned his canopy and bailed out.

"All this action had taken place below 3000 feet. As a matter of fact, the third combat wound up at 200 feet. So I went for altitude. As I climbed, Captain Davis and Lieutenant O'Nan joined me. The three of us started back for the bombers which were dropping their loads over Brunswick. We reached no more than 2000 feet when off to my left about twenty-five bandits in close formation going down through the clouds, appeared. The three of us immediately went in to attack, and followed them through the clouds. I found myself directly astern of a 190, which had a 109 right next to it. I evidently was unseen, as I got in a very successful burst at the 109, observing hits on the wings, fuselage and tail. The 109 caught fire and went straight into the ground.

"The 190 kept right on going as if nothing had happened to his wingman. He was a perfect duck to shoot at. I registered hits on his left wing, engine and canopy. The 190 went into a tight turn spiral and crashed."

Captured Focke-Wulf 190 in RAF markings at English base for testing. (RUST)

The attrition of a two-front war and years of combat were taking the toll of German pilots. While many of these intercepting formations, or gaggles as the Allied fighter pilots chose to call them, were led by veteran pilots who could give any American pilot and his Mustang a real run for his money, the ranks were being filled by youngsters who were very inadequately trained to enter combat. The long range of the Mustang created hostile skies over all the training fields of the Third Reich, and insured that fewer capable pilots would be coming up to meet them.

Regardless of their experience, it seemed that the Luftwaffe pilots just didn't want to believe the performance of the Mustang. Invariably they attempted to outclimb or outdive the P-51 as is exemplified in the combat of Lt. Joseph L. Lang of the 4th Fighter Group on May 24, 1944.

"Shortly after rendezvous we saw twenty plus Germans climbing 5000 to 6000 feet above us and at 12 o'clock to the bombers. We dropped tanks and climbed toward them. Some of them seeing us, split-essed away. Several 190s tried to come around behind us, but for some reason they broke away. I closed my section up astern to four Me 109s. I noticed another Mustang pull in front of one of the e/a (enemy aircraft). The P-51 was clobbered very badly and started losing altitude, smoking and burning. I closed on a 109 and fired. I missed and he broke down for the deck. At 35,000 feet, he started diving straight down. I fired and hit him in the starboard wing root and fuselage. I did this twice more. Most of the time he was rolling. At 18,000 feet, I noticed I had 650 to 675 on the clock. He started burning, then he shed his right wing.

"I leveled off at 2500 feet above some broken clouds and saw an FW 190 on the deck. I went down to attack. When I was 300 yards from him, I cleaned my tail and saw six FW 190s at 6 o'clock to me. I broke into them and was again bounced by a gaggle of twenty-five FW 190s.

"As there were three gaggles of twenty plus 190s, I had a busy time with them. When I saw I couldn't keep turning, I pushed everything to the gate and started climbing. They queued up in back of me and took turns shooting. Some of them kept climbing to the side of me and would make head-on passes at me. I finally hit some clouds at 18,000 feet and lost them. About fifteen to twenty FW 190s followed me to the clouds. I believe the Mustang will outclimb anything the German has."

Lt. Glenn Eagleston had one of the most unusual dogfights of his career when he dove his P-51 at 700 miles per hour in pursuit of a Focke-Wulf 190 which he finally destroyed.

"The Jerry thought I was another German at first," 'Eagle' said, "because he started rocking his wings. I was very friendly and rocked mine right back, moving in closer. Realizing his mistake, the Jerry turned into me as I gave him a burst. Then he rolled over and dived in an attempt to shake me.

"I salvoed my wing tanks and went down after him. He kept diving, but I knew I had the best ship and stayed right after him. He tried to pull out at 6000 feet, but his ship wouldn't take it and he spun into the ground.

"I pulled out at 8000 feet and glanced down at the airspeed indicator. I saw the needle quivering around the 700-mile-per-hour mark. And about that time, the wing tanks I dropped at 23,000 feet whizzed past, missing me by a mere foot or two."

The 4th Group set a new ETO record on April 8, 1944, with a rousing thirty-one victories scored for the loss of four Mustangs. The red-nosed P-51s thundered into Germany escorting the bombers to aircraft plants at Brunswick.

Blakeslee had just brought his unit to the rendezvous with the B-24 Liberators when he sighted the rising horde of enemy aircraft.

"Horseback to all Horseback aircraft. One hundred plus approaching bombers at 11 o'clock," he snapped.

The Mustangs dropped their tanks immediately and broke for the Germans, but not before the first wave of Luftwaffe fighters had dropped on the lead box of B-24s. Six of the lumbering bombers took fatal wounds from the onslaught. They seemed to lurch and stagger under the fire of their attackers and then they fell from formation streaming smoke and flame. Soon little wiggling objects could be observed emitting from the Liberators during their descent, and small white canopies popped out above them. Parachutes, smoke and debris seemed to fill the wake of the dying behemoths that plunged to their destruction.

Capt. Don Gentile, Capt. Louis Norley and Lieutenant Millikan picked out their targets and headed for them. Millikan got in a good deflection shot and sent his victim spinning to earth.

Norley caught a 190 at 2000 feet below him and chased it down to 3000 feet. The German did a tight climbing turn to the left, but Norley dumped 20 degrees of flap and turned inside him. As the Focke-Wulf rolled over and headed for the deck, Norley jumped right on top of him. Two short bursts and the German bailed out.

Norley pulled out and went after another 190 that was diving down below him. This one he chased for a mile or more before he pressed the gun button and saw the canopy of the 190 pop, followed by a somersaulting pilot.

The Mustang pilot then got in another turning match with a 190. He finally clamped on the enemy's tail, but overshot. Norley did a wingover and

B-17s of the Eighth Air Force over Norway. The Mustangs could take the "big friends" anywhere they could go. (USAF)

met the Focke-Wulf head-on. The 190 split-essed for the deck with the P-51 hot after him. The American blacked out in his pullout and recovered at 4000 feet, expecting to find the Jerry on his tail. But, alas, the 190 had flown into the ground and was splattered in smoldering ruins over the landscape. This gave Norley a triple for the day.

Other 4th Group pilots were meeting with equal success. Gentile knocked down three and Millikan got another before he tangled with a wily Luftwaffe veteran who fought him all over the skies over Brunswick. Tenaciously the two fighter pilots whirled round and round seeking an advantage. Finally the German spun out in a flaps-down turn. Before the pilot could recover, Millikan scored with a beautiful 90-degree deflection shot. The 109 burst into flames but the pilot managed to get out at about 800 feet. Just enough altitude for the chute to pop and save the German pilot to fight another day.

And so it went as the P-51s took the war home to the Third Reich. The bombers now went to targets with a minimum of losses to German fighters. In the meantime, Allied forces gathered in the armed camp that was England, awaiting the moment that they would hit the beach on the Continent and take the war to the Germans on the ground. The far-reaching bomber stream with its escort of high-stepping Mustangs helped to hasten that day.

B-24s of the Eighth Air Force let their bombs go. The Mustangs cut the losses of the bombers greatly. (USAF)

CHAPTER **4**

EIGHTH AND NINTH AF MUSTANGS

D-day and Beyond

ALL OF England had been abuzz since late spring of 1944 in expectation of the launching of the mightiest invasion fleet the world had ever known. Alert after alert had been called at the air bases, and the anxiety had reached a fever pitch. Finally the orders came; all men were restricted to base, and maintenance men worked around the clock to prepare aircraft for the big day. All available assistance was called in to assist in painting the broad black-and-white identity stripes on the wings and fuselages of each plane that would be flying over the beaches.

All through the night of June 5–6, the steady drone of engines filled the English skies as C-47s bearing paratroops and pulling gliders headed for Cherbourg Peninsula to deposit the vanguard of Allied troops on the Continent. Long before dawn, bombers rose to assemble in the murky skies before heading in to bomb enemy positions, and fighter-plane props began to turn shortly thereafter.

D-day was actually a great disappointment to the fighter pilots. For months they had anticipated the presence of hordes of Luftwaffe planes filling the arena to challenge the invasion. D-day would be the fighter pilot's dream; the enemy would be everywhere. Alas, such was not the case. Eighth Air Force Fighter Command flew seventy-three patrol and thirty-four fighter-bomber missions that day but the only enemy opposition that was

Mustangs of the 361st Fight Group in close formation. Note the P-51B in the lower corner and the fact that two of the P-51Ds are early models with no vertical-stabilizer fins. (USAF)

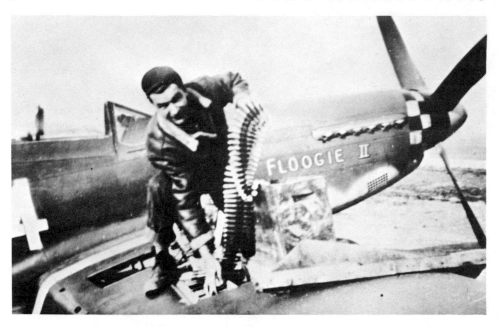

Loading the guns with .50-caliber rounds before a mission is an armorer of
the 357th Fighter Group. (OLMSTED)

encountered was in the interior of France. The Luftwaffe was as scarce as
hens' teeth over the beaches. Most of the Mustang pilots had to be satisfied
with attacks on ground targets of opportunity.

Once the Allied troops were firmly entrenched on the beachheads,
ground-support missions became more and more a part of the job of the
Mustangs. Of course this didn't detract from their primary mission of
escorting bombers, but with the arrival of new fighter units, more aircraft
became available for bombing and strafing.

As the infantry and armor struck forth to break out of the beachhead
peninsula, many P-51s were utilized to prevent German reinforcements
from reaching the combat area. Trains, railyards, tanks and trucks became
the primary targets of the many sorties that were flown in support of the
ground forces during the period shortly after the invasion.

All of these targets presented their own peculiar problems for the
Mustang pilots. Ample warning on the strafing of trains was given the pilots
of the 352nd Fighter Group by their commander, Col. Joe L. Mason in
these words: "On trains you always have the factor of a flak car being
present. They can be mean. It depends entirely on what kind of a train
you encounter as to what and how you handle the problem. Troop trains

are juicy but will always have one or two flak cars that must be taken care of. Tank cars burn very nicely. We started the idea of dropping half-full wing tanks into the side of wooden freight cars and the setting of gas on fire."

An unusual, yet highly successful, strafing mission along the lines of which Colonel Mason spoke was carried out by the 357th Fighter Group on June 16. Lt. Col. Thomas L. Hayes, Jr. led the unit which had been ordered to locate and strafe two trains between Poitiers and Angoulême in southern France. However, there was no information available as to their exact position, type or content. Another group was called and it was agreed that the 357th would arrive ten minutes before them, with each unit sweeping the area south.

Colonel Hayes found that the only auxiliary gas tanks available were 108-gallon capacity, so it was decided that the tanks would be filled and each pilot was instructed to fly only thirty minutes on each of the tanks which would leave them about two-thirds full. The tanks would then be used as fire bombs.

The 357th arrived a bit early and began dropping down to find a hole in the undercast over the area. To quote Colonel Hayes, "The only break in this cloud was the area from Poitiers to Angoulême, so I proceeded to search for trains. At the marshaling yard of Poitiers, rail transportation was seen. My top cover squadron, the 363rd, heard the conversation over the R/T, and when I started to lead down through a haze condition, they became separated and thought I was going down to attack. I was now leading the 364th and 362nd squadrons at 9000 feet, covering the railroad and main roads. Nothing was observed except a marshaling yard at St. Pierre, thirty miles south of Poitiers, with three lines of goods cars and other stray cars totaling one hundred cars in all. About one mile north, a train of thirty goods cars was rather neatly camouflaged by being parked between a cut of trees on a sharp bend. We flew south of Angoulême and observed congested traffic also at Angoulême, but I returned to St. Pierre as it looked like it was safe from flak.

"Having two squadrons now seemed to work smoothly and not too congested. As I mentioned before, the 363rd Squadron was raising hell at Poitiers at this time. Flying north on the sun side I left the 362nd at 9000 feet as top cover. I made a diving turn, slipping through some cloud at 3000 feet, and ended up on the deck, approaching the yard from the west or 90 degrees to it. My flight of four was slightly staggered abreast and coming in at 400 miles per hour, all firing ahead. As each one reached the cars, he released his tanks which sprayed the gasoline around. The

Maj. Pierce McKennon in the cockpit of P-51D "Ridge Runner." McKennon was an ace of the 4th Fighter Group. (WEATHERILL)

second flight, not far behind, fired into the bursted tanks, setting many of the cars on fire; and then in turn released their tanks as they passed over.

"My second section of eight Mustangs at this time splashed their tanks on the thirty cars one mile north. After setting them afire, the cars began to blow up. We all made one pass, strafing to increase damage and fire. Then we pulled up to cover the 362nd while they got in on the fun. This

A 363rd Fighter Group P-51B fitted with the English-designed Malcolm hood. (WEATHERILL)

second squadron picked out sections of cars and buildings still not burning. There was no use in strafing any more as the fires spread quickly. It was now that the Germans could see what was happening, and two flak cars started to fire, one on each side of the middle train. One element gave him two gas tanks while his wingman set the mess afire."

During the period of D-day and shortly thereafter, the new P-51Ds began to arrive in the theater. These new craft were an appreciable improvement over the P-51Bs, not only in that it incorporated the more powerful V-1650-7 engine, but also it was fitted with the new bubble canopy. The old greenhouse canopy of the P-51B had been the primary objection of the pilots since initial delivery of the aircraft for combat operations. The limited visibility in the earlier model had been partially improved in the fitting of the Malcolm hood on a number of P-51Bs operating out of England. The utilization of this English-manufactured canopy made a tremendous difference in the visibility of the pilot, and as a matter of fact, some of the men who flew Mustangs contend that even the P-51D with the bubble didn't give them the field of vision that they enjoyed with the Malcolm hood.

During this period, the first veteran P-38 group, the 55th, gave up its twin-engined aircraft for Mustangs. The transition was accomplished in good order, but the change from the torqueless P-38 to the P-51 did present its problems. However, the greatest difficulty experienced by the former Lightning pilots was unfamiliarity with fuselage tanks. With a full load, an unstable flight condition was created by the tank located right behind the pilot. The near-tragic consequences of the 55th, in transition due to this problem, is described by Maj. Edward B. Giller.

"Our first combat mission as a squadron flying P-51s with full internal and external tanks was a bit of a mess. I will never forget one incident. On climbing out from the base in full-squadron formation at 800 feet, the squadron in front of us had just pulled up into the lower cloud deck at 1000 feet when out of the bottom of the cloud came a spinning P-51. By some miracle of fate he dropped his tanks, recovered at about fifty feet with a permanently bent fuselage and in a very weak radio voice announced that he was aborting. I will never know to this day how he made the recovery. Needless to say, this unnerved the squadron, but everybody took a deep breath and climbed on into the soup. We made it to 25,000 feet but still had too much fuel in the fuselage tank. For some reason, at this point, a tight 360-degree turn was instigated which caused at least five to seven pilots to spin out. All of these dropped their tanks and recovered somewhere below."

The 343rd Fighter Squadron, 55th Fighter Group, flies above solid clouds as they return from an escort mission over Germany. (WEATHERILL)

After a bit of experience in the new single-engined fighters, such an occurrence became a thing of the past for the former P-38 pilots.

A week or so after D-day, the Germans began their attack on England with the introduction of the V-1, ramjet-propelled pilotless plane carrying a high-explosive warhead. Lt. William Y. Anderson of the 354th Fighter Group became one of the first Mustang pilots to shoot down one of the craft when he encountered a V-1 on June 17 on the way out to a dive-bombing mission. He clocked the speeding "bug" at 400 mph before he got in position behind it and pushed the gun button. The warhead exploded and Anderson was lucky to get away without damaging his plane. P-51 pilots destroyed a number of V-1s in a similar manner during the summer of 1944.

While Allied troops were fighting from hedgerow to hedgerow in the fields of Normandy, the bomber offensive against strategic targets in Germany went on relentlessly. A highlight of bomber operations in the ETO began on the morning of June 26. The 4th Fighter Group, led by Col. Don Blakeslee, and one squadron of the 352nd Fighter Group teamed up to escort 114 B-17s on the longest one-way trip thus far in the war. The P-51s took a lot of runway that morning laden with drop tanks filled to the brim. They would need every drop of fuel they could carry aloft, for their destination was Russia.

The Flying Forts dropped their bombs on the target at Ruhland and other than heavy flak, the mission met with no opposition until they got in the vicinity of Warsaw, Poland, where some ten to fifteen Me 109s showed up to block the way. The P-51s engaged them and they tucked their tails and fled, minus five of their number. After seven and a half hours flying time the 1600-mile journey came to an end. The Mustangs whipped around in steep banks and set down on the strip at Piryatin.

That night there was a great celebration; feasting and drinking of fiery vodka toasts with the Russians. However, unknown to them, a Heinkel bomber had followed the American formation, and the Luftwaffe would be out with a vengeance the following night. For the first time American P-51 pilots knew complete frustration as they came under heavy bombing attack. Quite a number of the Mustangs were destroyed, but they were lucky. At Poltava, the B-17s suffered appalling losses. Forty-three Flying Fortresses were destroyed on the ground.

The depleted force left Russia on June 26, with the bombers depositing their loads on Drohobycy, Poland, en route to AAF bases in Italy. After an uneventful mission the P-51s landed at Lucrera, in the land of the Fifteenth Air Force. The Eighth Air Force Mustangs were to see action when they joined the P-51s of the Fifteenth in escorting bombers to Budapest on July 2. The Luftwaffe rose to challenge and the 4th Group found itself in one heck of a dogfight. The outstanding performance of the day was turned in by Maj. H. D. "Deacon" Hively who shot down one 109 and then was hit in the canopy by another 109. Despite glass in one eye and bloodied vision, he fought back like a tiger to blast two more of the 109s and then make his way back to Italy.

A few days later, the fighter and bombers of the Eighth left Italy, flew an uneventful mission over France and returned to their respective English bases.

As Allied troops advanced into France, construction was begun immediately on advanced landing strips for their fighter support. One of the first units to move to the Continent was the Pioneer Mustang 354th Group. Upon their arrival in late June the unit wasted no time in beginning operations. In view of their close proximity to the lines, it was no problem for their Mustangs to fly six and eight missions a day.

On the afternoon of July 23, Lt. John S. Miller of the 354th was flying a sweep over the combat area when his Mustang was hit by flak. He stayed with the aircraft as long as possible, but it soon became evident that he would have to bail out. After leaving the cockpit he regained consciousness to find himself hung on the horizontal stabilizer, the leading edge lodged in his belly. With both hands he flipped the leading edge over his head, fell clear of the P-51 and reached for the rip cord. It wasn't

Mustangs of the 357th Fighter Group taxi out for takeoff. The external tanks on the wings gave them all the range they needed. (WEATHERILL)

there, and he spent anxious seconds locating it around on his back where it had slipped. Once found, he popped the chute and landed without great injury to himself.

The Mustangs of the Eighth Air Force, too, continued to give excellent cover to the Allied armored columns that were racing across France. Maj. John L. Elder of the 357th Fighter Group was shooting up a fortified town ahead of the advance when his P-51 was hit by flak. He swung away and over a hill, getting right down on the deck. Then a pair of flak towers opened up on him, scoring new hits on his plane. Seeing flashes all around, Elder flew over another hill but not before the enemy had put a hole in his cockpit canopy and knocked out his radio.

Flying at more than 300 mph, he suddenly realized that he was heading directly at a string of high-tension cables, but it was too late to pull up. Plowing right on through, Elder saw sparks and smoke fly all over the place as one of the cables swapped around his vertical stabilizer and rudder. The P-51 was hard to control, but it still hung together. Knowing he would have to bail out, Elder decided to try to get a little altitude, only to find himself over a German airfield which began pumping more lead at him.

By now, the Mustang was really heating up and Elder jettisoned his canopy and flew out over the French coast. He tried to get near Cherbourg to cut toward land where he could set his plane down on the beach, but everywhere he looked he saw flak. Shaking his head, he headed the Mustang back over the English Channel where he accomplished a successful ditching. He was picked up by Air-Sea Rescue and was returned to England none the worse for his dunking.

One of the sterling triumphs that the Mustangs helped accomplish in the weeks following D-day was complete air superiority over the Allied area. Very few American or British troops were even bombed or strafed by the Luftwaffe. Not only were the German attacks broken up in the air, but the enemy airfields were hit repeatedly.

When VIII Fighter Command first permitted the P-51 pilots to go down and strafe on return from their escort missions in the spring of 1944, it had been possible to surprise German airdromes, shoot up a few planes and get away scot free. After D-day, Luftwaffe airfields became virtual armed fortresses bristling with flak towers, multiple light batteries stationed around the area and men on alert to man them at all times. These targets took a great toll of American pilots during World War II and cost the lives of many more fighter aces than the Luftwaffe ever shot down.

These missions had to be carefully planned and expertly executed to keep casualties to a minimum. To attain this objective, Col. Don Blakeslee of the 4th Group had his own rules for airdrome strafing. They boiled down to three basic factors: surprise, speed and variation of the attack.

"I consider surprise as one of the chief factors in a successful strafe," said Blakeslee. "When my group is assigned to strafe a particular target, I ask for all photographs available. I want to know what the airfield looks like before I get there. I want my intelligence officer to get the best information he can of defense, and I want to know what kind and how many aircraft are reported to be on the field and where I can expect to find them parked. I also want to know what the terrain around the airdrome is.

"With this I can plan the approach best calculated to achieve surprise. I use terrain for cover and airdrome installations to screen my approach; I never come right in on an airdrome if I can help it. If I have planned to attack an airdrome beforehand, I pick an initial point some ten miles away. I have my course from there to the drome worked out. Once in the air, I take my boys right past the airdrome as if I had no intention of attacking at all. At my initial point I let down and wing back flat on the deck. Once I hit the drome, I really get down on the deck. I don't mean five feet up; I mean so low the grass is brushing the bottom of the scoop."

However, even the best of plans could not succeed without casualties. One of these was Maj. Don Beerbower, who was the leading ace of the 354th Group when he set out from the French airstrip on the afternoon of August 9. After making a pass on an airdrome about three miles north of Reims, drawing intense flak and seeing about thirty Ju 88s parked in revetments, Major Beerbower directed an attack in which he went in on the field from east to west as a diversion to draw fire, while the other flights went in from north to south to hit the enemy aircraft. Completely disregarding himself, Beerbower faced the concentrated flak in a diving attack, destroying a Ju 88 and knocking out two gun emplacements while effectively drawing the ground fire to his Mustang. While successful in diverting the fire from his other pilots, Beerbower's plane was hit again and again. He pulled up, jettisoned the canopy and attempted to bail out, but he was too low. The chute popped but never blossomed.

As Allied spearheads thrust forward in the direction of Paris, the 354th Group, along with the P-47 and P-38 units of the Ninth Air Force, continued to sweep the ground and the skies in front of them. On August 16, the Mustangs were on a fighter sweep over the German lines in the vicinity of Dreux, France, when the air controller reported that twenty Me 109s had been sighted. The P-51s immediately sped to intercept. As they moved to engage, another sixty German planes dropped out of the overcast some 3000 feet above them.

Lt. Ken Dahlberg and P-51B "Shillelaugh." Dahlberg was downed by German fighters, but he got three of them first. (DAHLBERG)

"I lived a lifetime in those few minutes," says Lt. Ken Dahlberg. "I clobbered one and he went straight into the ground burning. Everywhere you looked, there was a Mustang mixing it with three or four Jerries. I chandelled up into the midst of a gaggle of 109s. I picked one and tapped him. He blew up, showering my plane with oil and debris. My visibility was almost nil due to oil on my windshield, but I managed to make out a lone 109 and headed for him. Just then I noticed my oil pressure was down. Someone must have gotten on my tail and shot at me, but in the excitement I never knew it until then. My gunsight was also out, but by watching the tracer bullets I was able to spray the 109. He blew up. Four other 109s hopped my tail at the same time and I knew I had to bail out. I headed for the clouds so that Jerry wouldn't clobber me as I got out."

Once in the clouds, Ken went over the side and off into space. As quickly as he left his plane, the din of combat disappeared, and as his parachute opened, silence prevailed. Slowly he descended to land on the estate of a prominent French family—Dennis and Madeleine Baudoin.

Landing almost at the feet of Madame Baudoin, he had hardly

spilled his parachute when she rushed up to him. "Run and hide immediately," she told him. "This whole place is crawling with Germans."

Moving as swiftly as he could, he headed into the trees and brush and made his way to a stream. Quickly, he waded into the water and submerged his body until just his face was above the surface. Guttural words and sounds came to his ears as the German troops began to scour the grounds for the flier who had parachuted only a few minutes before. Resorting to a trick that many an American boy learned from Indian lore, he broke off a reed, put it in his mouth and ducked his head under water. Here he remained for what seemed an eternity while the search continued.

Dahlberg finally ventured to raise his head, but stuck close to the bank of the stream and made himself as inconspicuous as possible until night fell. Then he heard a low voice calling, and cautiously he crept from the water and moved to answer. It was Dennis Baudoin, the owner of the estate, who had brought him food. After hastily downing a belated meal, he was shown to a small tentlike structure made of twigs and sticks that was to be his hiding place during his stay.

Dahlberg was kept in hiding for several days, but with the news that American troops were nearing Paris, the young pilot implored Dennis Baudoin to help him go out to meet them. The two dressed in civilian attire and set out to find the Americans. In the confusion of retreating Germans, they went unchallenged. After a day of bicycling, a jubilant Dahlberg and his French companion came upon advancing U.S. troops.

Another Mustang pilot was downed over occupied France on August 18, but his rescue was accomplished in quite a different manner than that of Dahlberg.

"My plane has been hit by flak. I'm gonna belly it in," reported Capt. Bert Marshall, Jr. of the 355th Group.

Lt. Royce Priest, flying the Number Three position, pressed his R/T button, "Land in a road, coach," he said. "I'll land and pick you up."

There were protests over the R/T, protests and avowals, instructions and counterinstructions, but in the end Priest had his way. He soon realized that the field in which Marshall had landed was too soft to permit a landing which would enable him to take off again. But there was another field about three quarters of a mile away where some Frenchmen were loading hay onto a truck. The field was practically cleared of grain and on this section only short stubble remained.

Cutting his throttle almost to stalling speed, Priest landed in the stubble and braked to a halt. To make a runway, he whirled the plane around and rolled back to the eastern end of the field where he had first touched down.

Meanwhile, Marshall was running through plowed fields toward the plane. "It was tough going," he said. "I wasn't in shape for that stuff. I got pooped out. Every now and then I had to slow down to a fast walk. And I got kind of mad because I remembered I only had two American cigarettes and I didn't like the idea of sticking around in France with only two American cigarettes."

Priest turned the Mustang to the east once more, taxied out of the field, across the narrow road and into another hay field from which none of the

Lt. Royce Priest sits in the lap of Capt. Bert Marshall illustrating the manner in which they came home from France after the rescue mission. (MARSHALL)

shocks had been cleared. Marshall trotted up beside the plane. At that time a conversation transpired in which, as Priest recalls, "There was a reasonable amount of profanity involved."

Finally Priest stood up in the cockpit, hurled his parachute to the ground and said, "Get in!" Marshall shook his head disparagingly and climbed up and got into the seat.

Seated in Marshall's lap, Priest gave the plane the throttle and taxied back across the road to line himself up with his improvised runway. As the plane moved forward, the canopy slid back and struck Priest across the forehead. Marshall reached up with both hands and held it closed. At the end of the runway, Priest spied a large haystack and hauled the stick back into his stomach. They cleared the haystack by six inches.

The ride home was not the most comfortable the two ever had, but it was probably the happiest. The most surprised man was the tower operator when Priest called in to report his Mustang coming in for landing with two men aboard.

At least one other rescue of this type aboard a P-51 is recorded before several unsuccessful attempts were made. In view of the latter, orders were issued forbidding any further attempts of this nature.

Rapidly advancing armored columns and infantrymen had carried the war to the German frontier by the fall of 1944. Allied air power had increased to the point where 1000-plane raids on the Third Reich had become the ordinary rather than the exception. Practically all major targets were now in Germany, and the Luftwaffe had drawn in the majority of its forces to defend the cities of the fatherland. Great numbers of enemy aircraft came up on occasion to do battle with the American planes, and the Mustang pilots continued to take their toll.

It was on such a day that Lt. William R. Beyer of the 361st Fighter Group got five, using his new K-14 gunsight. The Mustangs were escorting the bombers to Kassel on September 27, 1944, when some forty of the enemy were sighted as they broke through the bombers and headed for the deck. Beyer picked out a group of about eight FW 190s and attacked them from above. Quickly he lined up on one and opened fire, closing from 400 to 100 yards. Good strikes were registered and the German pilot popped his canopy and spiraled off into a cloud. Beyer reefed into a tight 360 and then went down through the cloud to finish him off. Just as he broke through, he spotted a parachute off to his right. One down!

Picking up his wingman, Beyer spotted another 190 who did his best to get away by doing split-esses and tight turns, but the P-51 hung right with him. Then the German made the fatal mistake of attempting to climb. Beyer let fly, hit him and the pilot bailed out.

The Mustang pilot then pulled up and got on another 190 who absorbed one burst, called it quits, and went over the side.

Number four apparently had a bit more experience, for he led Beyer a merry chase for a few minutes and finally chopped his throttle and dropped his flaps in an attempt to get the American to overshoot. Beyer did likewise and fishtailed to keep from overshooting. The pilot of the 190 went into a gentle turn as the slugs from the P-51 began to rip into him. The pilot bailed out while still under fire.

The fifth 190 pulled up in a steep turn and then broke for the deck. Desperately he attempted to lose the Mustang on his tail and even tried to lead Beyer into some power lines. Beyer got up and over while the German

Capt. William T. Whisner holds up six fingers to announce his claim of six FW 190s on November 21, 1944. (USAF)

went under the wires. The P-51 was then right on top of him. Beyer opened up at only 75 yards and the 190 plowed into the ground and exploded.

Still the German planes continued to rise, even though these inexperienced pilots often seemed to blindly follow the leader and to make colossal blunders. The gaggle of 190s that Capt. Bill Whisner encountered southwest of Merseburg on November 21 didn't even bother to drop their tanks.

"Col. J. C. Meyer told me to take a straggler who was on the starboard and rear of the formation of 190s," related Whisner. "As I closed on him, the formation turned about 45 degrees right and this straggler joined the formation. I fired a short burst at this 190 at about 400 yards, using the K-14, but observed no strikes. I closed to 200 yards, fired another burst, which covered him with strikes. Large pieces flew off and he fell into a spin, smoking and burning.

"I closed on another 190 and hit him with a good burst from about 150 yards, knocking pieces off. He fell off to the right and I hit him again at 15 to 20 degrees deflection from 100 yards or less. Again pieces came off and he fell into a flat spin. I watched this one go through a haze layer, still spinning and smoking. About this time the enemy seemed to be worried. I saw two of them break off and dive down, taking violent evasive action. I did not attempt to follow them, but stayed behind the formation.

"I closed up behind a three-ship flight which was flying almost line abreast, about 50 yards apart. I put my sight on the leader but before I opened fire, he broke down. I was then almost between the other two. I banked steeply to the right, then back to the left and hit the one on the right at less than 100 yards. Pieces flew off him and he fell off into a flat spin, smoking and burning.

"I was depending on my wingman, Lieutenant Waldron, to get the one on the left and he didn't fail me. I saw him hit the 190 which went down out of control, smoking.

"I closed on another 190 which was turning from left to right. He saw me and turned steeply to the right. I cut him off and hit him all over in a deflection shot of 15–20 degrees at 200 yards or less. He went in a vertical dive, puffing smoke and flame, and disappeared into the haze. At this time I saw another 190 going down. My wingman had gotten this one.

"I made a 180-degree turn right while watching him, and lost my wingman. The main formation of 190s was still intact, but only two planes remained in the other section. I fire walled everything and caught up surprisingly fast. I picked the last one, fired at him from 300 yards. Being slightly below, and due to the heavy contrails, I did not see any strikes on him. He snapped into a tight spin and went below me. I claim a probable on this one.

Two Mustangs of the 353rd Fighter Group fly formation with one of the bombers that they escorted so well. (RUST)

"I was very close to the main formation at this time. I picked out one of them and started firing from about 200 yards. He was completely covered with strikes and fell off into a dive. I turned and watched him and he broke into several pieces. I think his belly tank exploded. Up to this time, none of the 190s had dropped their belly tanks. I had plenty of time to plan my attacks and those tanks made the 190s extremely vulnerable. As I fired on this last one, the main formation dropped their tanks and dived down and to the left. I followed, but lost them in the haze. As I pulled up, I saw three of the 190s behind me, so I stood my plane on its tail and lost them.

"At about 23,000 feet I saw a 190 on a P-51's tail. I attacked him and fired a deflection shot from 100 yards. As I mushed past his line of flight, he flew through my fire. He then leveled out and I hit him from slightly above at 50 yards. My fire hit him in the cockpit and engine. His canopy flew off along with other large pieces. He went straight down with his engine burning and smoking. I joined Colonel Meyer and came out with them."

For his claim of six destroyed and one probable, Whisner was awarded five destroyed and two probables.

Multiple claims were many during the fall and winter days of the gaggles. In addition to the two combats just described, several other Mustang

*353rd Fighter Group Mustang
waits on taxi strip while another P-51
comes in for landing.* (TANNER)

*"Double Trouble" of the
352nd Fighter Squadron,
353rd Fighter Group. Drop tanks
in place.* (RUST)

pilots scored five victories on one mission during this period. They were Capt. C. E. "Chuck" Yeager of the 357th Group on October 22; Capt. Donald S. Bryan of the 352nd Group on November 2; Lt. Claude J. Crenshaw of the 359th Group on November 21; Capt. L. K. "Kit" Carson of the 357th Group on November 27; Lt. J. S. Daniel of the 339th Group on November 26 and Capt. William J. Hovde of the 355th Group on December 2.

On the ground, the German resistance became tenacious once the fatherland was invaded. Allied troops, who had raced through France, encountered very stiff opposition at the Siegfried Line. Hopes for an end to the war in Europe in 1944 were dashed, and with the advent of winter, the lines became static.

Under the cover of unseasonably bad weather, the Germans assembled their forces for a final, desperate offensive against the Allied forces. In the early morning of December 16, 1944, German panzer divisions, strongly supported by infantry, struck along a line between Monschau and Krewinkel, Germany. Swiftly, the onrushing German armor rolled into Luxembourg and Belgium. Desperately the Allies fought a retreating action to delay the enemy until reinforcements could be rushed forward to plug the gap.

The weather all but forced the Allied air forces from the skies, and missions in support of the beleaguered troops were kept to a minimum. However, Allied fighter units were rushed to advanced bases on the Continent. Among these were the 352nd and 361st Fighter Groups of the Eighth Air Force whose Mustangs arrived in Belgium on December 23.

These units went into action immediately, as Eighth and Ninth Air Force fighters and bombers utilized the first break in the weather to hammer the German ground forces unmercifully.

It was on a support mission, while flying from the 352nd's advanced base at Asch, Belgium, that Maj. George Preddy, holder of the ETO record of six victories on one mission on August 6, 1944, met a tragic fate on Christmas Day 1944. While on patrol, enemy aircraft were reported in the vicinity of Coblenz. Preddy led his squadron to the position, spotted the enemy and turned into the attack. The Mustang pilot had just begun to gain an advantage in a turning match when another Me 109 cut in front of him. A short burst from Preddy's guns found its mark and the pilot bailed out.

The all-time-scoring Mustang ace, Maj. George Preddy of the 352nd Fighter Group. (SAFFRO *via* HILL)

He then went back to his original opponent and bested him again. Once on the tail of the 109, a long burst produced numerous hits and again the pilot bailed out.

Preddy then received a new report of bandits in the area and this time he and two other P-51s headed for Liège, Belgium. As they approached, an FW 190 was spotted at about 1500 feet. The Focke-Wulf broke for the deck with the 352nd Group ace right on his tail. As he closed the distance to get in firing range, American antiaircraft opened up. The German fighter raced through the barrage, but as Preddy attempted to break off and get out of the fire, he was hit repeatedly. The Mustang went up in a sharp chandelle, staggered and fell to the ground. The top-scoring Mustang ace of the ETO had fallen to friendly fire.

Through the use of airpower, the dogged resistance of the Allied troops was further enhanced to the point of stopping the German offensive in its tracks. The infamous "Battle of the Bulge" was over. By the end of December the full brunt of the German attack had been defeated.

The 352nd Group continued to operate from Asch throughout the German offensive, and was in a position to intercept on January 1, 1945,

"Petie 2nd," the P-51D flown by Lt. Col. John C. Meyer during many of his victories with the 352nd Fighter Group. (MEYER)

when the Luftwaffe made an all-out strike on Allied air bases in Belgium and Holland. Over seven hundred German fighters came in, skimming the ground, and wrought great destruction to many of the bases. The one bright spot for the Americans that day was the effort of the 487th Fighter Squadron of Mustangs. With Lt. Col. John C. Meyer leading, twelve P-51s took off into the face of a strafing attack by fifty Me 109s and FW 190s.

One of the primary pilots involved in the air battle was Capt. Bill Whisner. "After shooting down that first 190, I felt myself being hit," he said. "I had several 20-mm holes in each wing and another hit in the oil tank. My left aileron control was also out and I was losing oil, but my pressure and temperature were steady. Being over friendly territory, I could see no reason for landing immediately, so I turned toward a big dogfight and shortly had another 190 in my sights. It went down with the pilot in it. The plane exploded and burned when it hit the ground.

"There were several 109s in the vicinity, so I engaged one of them. We fought for five or ten minutes and I finally managed to get behind the German. I hit the plane good and saw the pilot bail out from 200 feet. His plane landed in the vicinity of fifteen or twenty others which had already been blasted out of the sky. My last victim, another 109, was trying to strafe an American airstrip. I landed strikes in the nose and wings of the 109 and saw it crash east of the strip.

"I chased several more of the enemy, but they got away in the clouds. By then I could hardly see as my windshield and canopy were covered with oil."

When things settled down over the base, Whisner came in for a safe landing.

Lt. Col. John C. Meyer and the eleven pilots from the 487th tallied twenty-three victories that morning. Leading the scoring were Whisner and Capt. Sanford K. Moats with four each. Capt. Raymond H. Littge and Lt. Col. Meyer each got two. This feat was accomplished without the loss of a single Mustang pilot. For their victory, the 487th was awarded the Distinguished Unit Citation, the only fighter squadron in the ETO to be so honored.

The Luftwaffe left thirty AAF and one hundred and twenty RAF planes destroyed on the ground that day, but the price that they paid is indicative of their failure. Over two hundred German fighters fell to Allied air and ground defenses.

By the spring of 1945, Nazi Germany lay in ruins. Allied ground forces pushed forward into Germany and seized the industrial Ruhr Valley. Tanks and infantrymen steadily fought their way toward the Rhine River

Formation of Mustangs of the 353rd Fighter Group illustrating the effect
olive-drab painting of upper surfaces. (TANNER

Unusual markings and paint job feature this P-51D of the 55th Fighter Group
(USAF)

Beautiful side view of the 364th Fighter Group's "Penny"
flown by Lt. Col. John W. Lowell. (HILL)

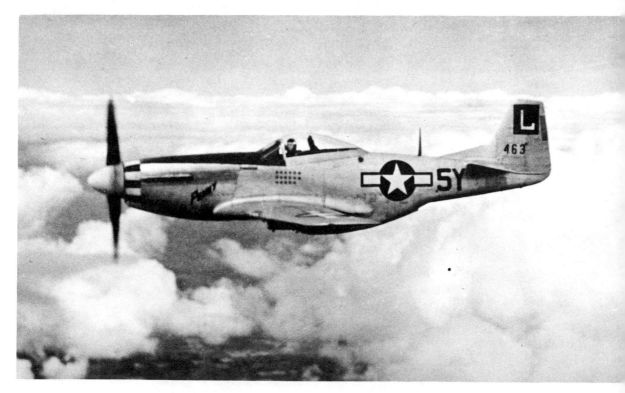

and Berlin. Allied airpower so dominated the skies that their formations were overhead at all hours. Appearance of the Luftwaffe was sporadic and other than the jet threat, which is the subject of the next chapter, presented no great challenge.

It was not unusual for American fighters to sight bombers and cargo aircraft making mad dashes from one beleaguered airfield to another, so disrupted were the German communications and transportation systems. Many German military staff members and military dispatch couriers were forced to make use of the air rather than chance the highways which were constantly being strafed. Bomber types which American fighter pilots had never seen took to the air in these missions, as well as to make hit-and-run attacks on rapidly advancing Allied armored columns.

Capt. C. B. East and Lt. Lee Larson of the 15th Tactical Reconnaissance Squadron were on an armed reconnaissance mission in the vicinity of Wittenberg when they sighted a Junkers Ju 88 bomber. Captain East made the first pass, firing from 500 to 100 yards, scoring hits on the fuselage and setting the left engine on fire. Larson attacked from the other side and when he broke off, the right engine was burning. The big twin-engined craft went into a gentle glide. One man bailed out before the Junkers exploded.

An hour later, the two pilots sighted an FW 190 flying west at 2000 feet and opened fire at 100 yards. The Focke-Wulf crashed and burned. These encounters had no effect over the primary mission of the Mustang pilots. Captain East returned to file a thorough report on all marshaling yards and rail lines on his route.

Strategic-bombing missions continued relentlessly until the very end of the war in Europe. As long as the Fortresses and Liberators struck at the heart of Germany, the P-51s continued to escort them.

Lt. Col. Sid Woods was leading the 4th Fighter Group, in the vicinity of Berlin on March 22, 1945, when he sighted four bombed-up FW 190s heading for the Russian lines. Immediately he closed on the No. 4 man in the flight, gave him a burst and observed him nose over and hit the deck.

Woods then found himself under attack from another 190 coming in from his left at 90 degrees. He shoved the stick down and let him pass over. The P-51 pilot then pulled straight up, rolled off the top and came down on his tail. The 190 went into an aileron roll, with the P-51 firing away. With both aircraft on their backs, the 190 took hits and nosed down to crash on Fürstenwalde airdrome.

Woods then caught another flight of four turning between Eggersdorf and Fürstenwalde airdromes. He tapped the No. 4 man with a two-second

Even the enemy could not mistake the "Ace" insignia on the Mustang cowling of Capt. Don Bochkay's Mustang. (WEATHERILL)

burst. The German immediately salvoed his bombs, jettisoned the canopy and went over the side.

Then the Mustang pilot sighted two 190s on the tail of a P-51 and he dived down to hit one flying right above the ground. He flew right on into it.

Climbing to 3000 feet the 4th Group commander sighted another flight of four. Again he chose to close on No. 4, but as he came in on his tail, all of the Focke-Wulfs broke violently to the left. Woods racked in so tight that his gyro spilled, so he had to give deflection with his fixed sight. As the German pulled into a steep climbing turn, the tracers caught him and strikes could be seen all over the cockpit. The craft caught fire, crashed and burned.

The Mustangs of the Ninth Air Force's 354th Group were operating from a strip in northern France in the spring of 1945. Their proximity to the fighting front enabled them to fly many types of tactical missions as well as to escort bombers when the occasion arose.

Lt. Andrew J. Ritchey, with Lieutenant Salter flying his wing, was dispatched on a weather reconnaissance mission on April 2. The two Pioneer Mustang Group pilots sighted two FW 190s over Erfurt airdrome, preparing to land. Both P-51s dived down, firing. Both of the 190s crashed onto the airfield.

Lieutenants Ritchey and Salter then sallied forth over Gotha airdrome where they shot down one FW 190 which was flying at 3000 feet. Immediately after this encounter they saw ninety plus FW 190s and Me 109s in

Lt. Col. Glenn T. Eagleston, top-scoring ace of the Ninth Air Force. He accounted for 18½ e/a, flying with the 354th "Pioneer Mustang" Group. (USAF)

waves of eight, flying west at 3000 feet. Most of them were carrying belly tanks, apparently intent on destroying some of the equipment being rushed to advancing Allied forces. The two Mustangs bounced the first two formations, claiming one FW 190 destroyed, one damaged and one Me 109 destroyed. Low on fuel and ammunition, the Americans headed for home with their "weather report."

Due to lack of fuel and replacement parts for their aircraft, most of the Luftwaffe was grounded by the middle of April 1945. The fighter units of the Allies took advantage of this position and sent out many strafing missions to destroy these craft and their airdromes as well. Though some of the airfields were deserted and the planes unfueled, most were still manned and the flak batteries as active as ever. Such was the airdrome that Maj. Edward B. Giller and members of the 55th Group attacked on the afternoon of April 16.

"Since the number of targets in the area (Brunnthal airdrome) was not lucrative enough to engage the entire squadron, I released the flights to find their own targets," stated Giller. "I broke my white flight down into the elements to cover this area. My wingman, Lieutenant Arnold, and I made our passes parallel with the autobahn, from south to north, clobbering the aircraft which were parked in the woods along either side of the road. My first attack was on a Heinkel He 111; I gave it a pretty good squirt and observed many strikes on it. It started to burn in a beautiful burst of flames.

Crew chiefs guide the Mustangs as the 370th Fighter G
taxi out for a mission in 1945. (U₅

"Parked just beyond the He 111 was an Me 109. I put the pipper on it, getting a good concentration of hits. Just as I pulled up over it, a steady stream of black smoke began to belch forth from it.

"I had seen two other aircraft parked in this same area on the east side of the road during this first pass, so I went in again, making the same pattern from south to north. The first aircraft turned out to be a Junkers 52 parked a little farther back from the road than my first two targets. I fired at it, pretty well covering the engines; it burst into flames. I had to make a third pass to position myself on the fourth target which I had observed. It was a Ju 88. I came in on the same pattern, and although I observed many strikes, it would not burn. As I pulled up from this last pass, a 20-mm flak shell came in the left side of my canopy and exploded, wounding me in the left shoulder. I was dazed and bleeding rather badly, so I called my flight together and went home."

Thousands of German aircraft were destroyed in a similar manner during the final days of the Third Reich. As Allied tanks and troops pulled up to a standstill, P-51s continued to range over Germany until the very end.

In all probability the last Mustang victories in the ETO were scored on May 8, 1945, by Lieutenants Lee Larson and Schroeder when they performed the unusual feat of destroying two Focke-Wulf 190s without firing a shot. The section approached the planes with the intention of escorting them back to base with them. The 190s took hostile action and the two Mustangs reacted. Schroeder followed one which hit the deck at a suicide altitude, and followed it until it crashed into the trees.

Larson fastened himself to the tail of the other. The 190 dived to 500 feet, made a tight turn to the left, spun out and crashed into the ground.

"Angels' Playmate," the P-51D of Capt. Bruce Carr, Ninth Air Force ace, on display in Paris after World War II. (E. C. ARMESS)

The only shots were those fired by the Germans in their first hostile action. They scored a single hit in Schroeder's left wing.

From December 1943 until V-E Day on May 8, 1945, the Mustangs had taken the war to the depths of Germany. They had fought the best that the Luftwaffe could put into the skies and beaten it down to the ground. Not a square foot of the defeated Third Reich was safe from their guns and bombs. The high-pitched whine of the Merlins sang a song of victory as the silver Mustangs headed home from their last day of combat over Europe.

CHAPTER 5

THE EIGHTH AND NINTH VS. THE GERMAN JETS

T H E appearance of the German jets in 1944 came as no great surprise to Allied Intelligence. Since 1943 they had been aware that the Luftwaffe possessed such craft and were striving to make them operational. The Messerschmitt Me 163 (actually a rocket-driven interceptor burning hydrogen-peroxide and water with hydrazine hydrate and methyl alcohol for a catalyst) and the Messerschmitt Me 262 had been in stages of development for some years and RAF photo reconnaissance had been keeping tab on their bases for some time. The initial test of the Me 262 had been so successful that Gen. Adolf Galland, Chief of Luftwaffe Fighter Forces, had requested that other fighter production be curtailed in order that more resources and attention could be devoted to the craft. Unfortunately for the Luftwaffe and fortunately for the Allies, Hitler decreed that the Me 262 be developed as a bomber! This resulted in at least a four-month delay in making the aircraft tactically operational, much to the chagrin of the German fighter pilots.

Col. Avelin P. Tacon, Jr. was leading his green-nosed Mustangs in the vicinity of Merseburg, Germany, on the twenty-eighth of July when he encountered two Me 163s. One of his pilots called out two contrails heading for the bomber stream, so Tacon put his flight into a 180-degree turn to meet the interceptors head-on. Once the Mustangs were sighted, the Me 163s split up, one diving rapidly toward the ground and the other pulled up into the sun, his rocket engine blowing defiant smoke rings at the pursuing Americans.

The impact of this encounter is indicated by the following extract

The rocket-powered Messerschmitt Me 163 scored some initial success over the Eighth Air Force bombers, but had too many difficulties of its own to be an effective opponent. (USAF)

from a TWX sent out by Maj. Gen. William Kepner, Commander of the VIII Fighter Command, the same day:

> . . . . IT IS BELIEVED THAT WE CAN EXPECT TO SEE MORE OF THESE AIRCRAFT IMMEDIATELY AND THAT WE CAN EXPECT ATTACKS ON BOMBERS FROM THE REAR IN FORMATIONS OF WAVES. TO BE ABLE TO COUNTER AND HAVE TIME TO TURN INTO THEM OUR UNITS ARE GOING TO HAVE TO BE IN POSITIONS RELATIVELY CLOSE TO THE BOMBERS TO BE BETWEEN THEM AND OUR HEAVIES. IT IS BELIEVED THESE TACTICS WILL KEEP THEM FROM MAKING EFFECTIVE, REPEAT EFFECTIVE, ATTACKS ON THE BOMBERS. ATTENTION IS CALLED TO THE FACT THAT PROBABLY THE FIRST THING SEEN WILL BE HEAVY, DENSE CONTRAILS HIGH AND PROBABLY 30,000 FEET AND ABOVE APPROACHING REAR OF THE BOMBERS. JET AIRCRAFT CAN ESPECIALLY BE EXPECTED IN LEIPZIG AND MUNICH AREA OR ANY PLACE EAST OF NINE DEGREE LINE.

The Messerschmitt Me 262 which posed a great threat to the American bombers over Germany and presented the Mustang with one of its greatest challenges. (USAF)

General Kepner was not the only one excited about the event. The appearance of the jets brought VIII Bomber Command face to face with a new dilemma. Would the escorting Mustangs be able to cope with all-out attacks from the new aircraft or would their speed present them with such a problem that bomber losses would again become so large as to be prohibitive. This was the moot question of the day and the greatest test of combat which had ever confronted the indomitable Mustangs!

The problem was intensified with the first real success of the German jets on August 5, 1944. On missions flown that day, the VIII Bomber Command lost three aircraft to the enemy's jet craft, and in an attempt to protect the bombers, three Mustangs fell victim to Me 163s. The jets dove down on them from above in trail and pressed their attacks to point-blank range, then the craft zoomed into the sky above. The three Mustangs caught fire and fell earthward.

On August 16 a Mustang registered its first kill over one of the vaunted new Luftwaffe aircraft. Lt. Col. John B. Murphy of the 359th Fighter Group was flying escort in the Leipzig area when the bombers came under attack from Me 163s. One of the tiny craft cut his power and dived upon a straggling B-17 and Murphy pushed everything to the fire wall to try to close the gap. Although he was indicating over 400 mph, the jet still had time to overshoot the bomber before the Mustang got his chance.

As the Me 163 flattened out of his dive, Murphy opened fire at 1000 feet and closed to point-blank range, getting strikes on the tail and left side of the fuselage before he overshot and had to pull off to the side. His wingman, Lt. Cyril Jones, closed in and took a shot from slightly beneath and the enemy fighter split-essed and headed down with Jones still getting strikes. However, he hit the wash from the jet and blacked out, so they had to settle for a damaged claim on the enemy plane.

The initial victory was not long in coming, for when Lieutenant Colonel Murphy pulled out of his climbing turn, he sighted another Me 163 circling off to his left, 5000 feet below. Diving down, he came inside the circle of the jet and fired, closing rapidly. Hits on the left side of the fuselage caused a large explosion and the whole rear of the fuselage blew off. The Mustang had scored its first triumph over a jet!

Most jet contacts up until October 1944 had been with the rocket-powered Me 163. At the insistence of Reichsmarshal Hermann Goering and fighter commanders in the Luftwaffe, two Jager-Erprobungskommandos of Messerschmitt 262s were formed under the able leadership of Maj. Walter Nowotny, a 250-victory ace. A total of some thirty aircraft were assigned to the unit which was based at Achmer and Hesepe near Osnabrück, Germany.

An ill omen for the Luftwaffe and sign of the tactics to come was demonstrated by Mustang pilot Lt. Urban L. Drew of the 361st Fighter Group on October 7. On this day he caught two Me 262s taking off from their base at Achmer, and using his decided advantage of speed and altitude, dove down on his prey to destroy both of them.

That same day, American fighter ace Colonel Hubert Zemke, who had immortalized himself flying P-47s as commander of the famed 56th Fighter Group, chalked up an Me 262 while flying a Mustang. Zemke, who had recently taken over the 479th Fighter Group of the Eighth Air Force, encountered an enemy aircraft while flying in spotty weather in the vicinity of Nordhausen. Zemke and his wingman, Lt. Norman Benolt, attacked what they thought was a Messerschmitt 109. They obtained good strikes at long range and the left wing of the craft broke off in a dive at 520 mph at 10,000 feet. On their return to base they filed a claim for the destruction of one Me 109 shared. Evaluation of their film definitely identified the aircraft destroyed as an Me 262 and not a propeller-driven plane as originally believed. So, unknowingly, the two pilots had become early victors over the vaunted German jet.

The superior high-speed performance of even a lone Me 262 was demonstrated in a wild-and-wooly air encounter on the afternoon of November 1. The B-17s of the Eighth Air Force had been on a mission to the synthetic-oil refinery at Gelsenkirchen with little opposition, and were on their way home via Holland when they were intercepted by one of the jet fighters piloted by Oberfähnrich Banzhaff. Approaching at 38,000 feet the Luftwaffe pilot nosed his plane into a dive toward the top cover section of Mustangs from the 20th Fighter Group. Down he came in a perfect dive and quickly he lined up on the No. 4 man of the formation and shot him down in flames.

He continued his dive over the Fortress formation with Mustangs in hot pursuit. Leveling out at 1000 feet, Banzhaff made a climbing 180-degree turn at full throttle, taking up a northerly heading toward the Zuyder Zee just above a cloud layer. Had he ducked into the clouds he would have gotten off scot free, but he apparently decided that his superior speed was enough to see him through. This was a fatal mistake, for it gave an assortment of Mustangs and Thunderbolts from three different fighter groups a chance to cut him off.

Both types of aircraft opened fire on him, getting hits on the left side of the fuselage and the left wing. Lt. Dick Flowers of the 20th Fighter

A Messerschmitt Me 262 in French markings after making a belly landing after World War II. (E. C. ARMESS)

Head-on view of the French-liberated Me 262. Note pitot tube and gun ports in the nose. (E. C. ARMESS)

Group got strikes in his screaming Mustang which was pulling 72 inches of mercury at 3000 rph, as did Lieutenant Gerbe of the 352nd Fighter Group. Once the jet had made the mistake of letting the Americans catch him, there was no hope for him to try to outmaneuver them. In desperation, Banzhaff made a climbing turn to the left and Lieutenant Groce, a 56th Group P-47 pilot, easily pulled his nose right through the jet in order to get enough deflection, firing all the time. The jet's right engine burst into flames and the plane fell off into a spin. The pilot bailed out.

Six pilots had been involved in downing the jet, but it was subsequently awarded to Mustang pilot, Lieutenant Gerbe and Thunderbolt pilot, Lieutenant Groce, on an equal basis.

In view of the superior speed of the Me 262, the Mustang pilots quickly realized that they must develop air-to-air tactics to combat the craft. Altitude and maneuverability were essential countermeasures. To attack the jet, the P-51 needed to initiate a diving attack to gain closure speed on the enemy aircraft. Only in this manner could the Mustang pilots get in striking range of the jets when they attacked the bombers. If attacked, the P-51 could easily turn and maneuver inside the turning radius of the Me 262. This put them in a position to meet the jet head-on or to get in a shot if the enemy overran them in his attack. The P-51 pilot was actually in a much better position to defend himself than he was to divert the swift attacks of the jets upon the bombers.

Kommando Nowotny saw its last action on the eighth of November when it lost four aircraft, including its leader. At least three of these fell to Mustangs. Lt. James W. Kenney of the 352nd Fighter Group was escorting a fellow pilot who was experiencing engine trouble back to England when they met a formation of unescorted B-17s. Kenney decided that if his comrade's aircraft could make it they would tag along with the bombers for a short time. During this period, Lt. Franz Schall in his Me 262 attacked the Fortresses and came back past the P-51s. Kenney turned to the attack and was able to get in a good burst from a 90-degree position as the jet came winging past. Strikes were registered all over the jet's left wing and engine.

At this time Schall reported to his ground control that his throttles were jammed, apparently he didn't realize that his engine was smoking badly. Struggling to regain power, he glanced back to discover that two Mustangs were sitting on his tail. Fully realizing his hopeless plight, he chose to jettison the canopy and hit the silk.

Another Me 262 was shared by two Mustang pilots, Capt. Ernest C. Fiebelkorn of the 20th Fighter Group and an unidentified flier from possibly the 357th Group. Just as both pilots lined up for the kill, the jet spun in and exploded without either firing a shot.

Perhaps the most decisive Me 262 loss occurred when Major Nowotny went down in flames. It is known that he attacked a formation of bombers and that he in turn was intercepted by Mustangs. His last radio transmissions reported, "Just made the third kill . . . Left jet has failed . . . been attacked again . . . been hit." Seconds later his Me 262 came screaming down and crashed in flames six kilometers north of Bramsche.

After this air battle, Gen. Adolf Galland gave the order to dissolve the Kommando for reorganization. During the period of October 1 to November 8, 1944, the unit had been credited with the destruction of twenty-two Allied aircraft.

The remaining pilots of the unit were to form the nucleus of the first jet fighter wing, J.G. 7, which would be led by another high-scoring Luftwaffe ace, Maj. Theo Weissenberger. By late December it was in position as I/J.G. 7 at Brandenburg-Briest; II/J.G. 7 at Neumünster and III/J.G. 7 at Parchim.

Although few jets were encountered for the balance of 1944, fighter commanders were aware of the problems that these aircraft would present to the bomber formations once spring and good flying weather began to prevail. One such commander who was hard at work on a solution to the dilemma was Lt. Col. William C. Clark who had just taken over the 339th Fighter Group of the Eighth Air Force. With the able assistance of some of his veteran pilots, Colonel Clark began researching all possible information relating to the Me 262. Where and how it was built, where they were based and how pilots were trained, where their fuel came from, etc.

Then the three known air bases of the jets were selected for special study. Photos of the fields provided valuable information concerning the general terrain and defenses, and best low-altitude approaches were determined. The general idea was to flush the 262s and to shoot them down as they attempted to take off. If the aircraft refused to rise to the bait, then the air bases would be strafed and as many of the jets destroyed on the grounds as possible. In addition, the bases would be shot up to such a degree as to render them unserviceable.

One squadron of Mustangs would be left high in the air as top cover for the strafers if any airborne Me 262s got away. Another flight of eight Mustangs would be left loitering in the area to get any escapees who tried to come home to roost.

In the spring of 1945 Colonel Clark was to put these tactics to use with great effect. To what extent is best described by Clark, "Of the three air bases we picked, we were able to attack two. One of the first (just northwest of Berlin), we claimed and were awarded three destroyed and two damaged in the air. We found out later that we had chased six more north to the Baltic where they flamed out and were lost. We never got credit for these, of course. One more tried to land at the base after our last flight had left but flamed out off the end of the runway and crashed.

"The air base was so badly damaged that it never became operational again. I inspected it myself after the war and found that no repair work had been done after we left it. A Luftwaffe officer told me that we set their fuel supply on fire and they could get no more. Two Me 262s which survived the attacks were put in storage.

"We didn't lose a single airplane on this operation. I am more proud of this fact than anything else. On three planned missions (March 20, March 30 and April 3, 1945) we were credited with eight destroyed, one probable and five damaged in the air; twenty-six destroyed on the ground, and probably caused the destruction of that many more without a loss of our own."

The effectiveness of catching the Me 262s on takeoff is expressed in the combat-encounter report of Capt. Donald M. Cummings of the 55th Fighter Group who got two on February 25, 1945.

"I was leading Hellcat Yellow Flight on a fighter sweep at 10,000 feet in the vicinity of Giebelstadt airdrome when several Me 262s were called in at 2 o'clock, taking off from the field. Captain Penn, the squadron leader, ordered us to drop our tanks and engage. I peeled off from 10,000 feet making a 180-degree turn to the left in a 70-degree dive after a jet which was then approaching the airdrome. I commenced firing from 1000 yards in a steep diving pass and after about three seconds observed many strikes. Since I was closing fast and approaching the airfield, which was beginning to throw up intense and accurate flak, I broke left and up, taking evasive action when about one third of the way across the field. My wingman, who was behind me, saw the 262 touch ground, cartwheel and burn."

The last claim against the erratic Me 163 was scored on March 15, 1945, in the Leipzig-Kassel area. Capt. Ray S. Wetmore of the 359th Group was credited with one of the craft when it attempted to intercept the bomber stream. While the Me 163s gained much publicity, it is doubtful that they actually downed over a dozen Allied aircraft during the war. The extreme danger of operation of this rocket-powered plane and its very short endurance in the air handicapped the Me 163 extensively.

The Mustangs continued to encounter and harass the Me 262s as the war in Europe drew closer to an end. Maj. Edward B. Giller was one

The first twin jet ever to enter combat was the Arado 234. However, its bombing proved to be ineffective and it was an easy prey to the P-51. (WRIGHT FIELD)

Lt. Col. John C. Meyer accounted for the first Arado 234 twin jet. Meyer scored twenty-one aerial victories flying Mustangs. (USAF)

of those who caught one of the jets trying to return to his home base. On the afternoon of April 9, 1945, Giller sighted a 262 at 24,000 feet in the Munich area. Two other Mustangs took off chasing him and after about ten minutes Giller managed to cut him off after the other two gave up the chase. He stayed with the jet as he began to let down south of the city.

"I lost him again for a minute, then discovered him making for Munich/Riem airdrome," Giller recalled. "I didn't know if he was going to land or try to drag me over some flak. Going 'balls out' I caught him at fifty feet just over the perimeter track. He was going west to east about 100 yards to the right of the runway. I fired several bursts and observed strikes on the left-wing root and fuselage. I noticed his wheels were not down and his airspeed was about 200 mph. As my speed was about 450, I overshot rapidly and pulled up. When I looked back, I saw him crash-land or belly in on the field 100 yards to the right of the runway in a large cloud of dust and flying pieces. He did not burn, which I believe was due to the fact that he was out of fuel. The aircraft was completely wrecked."

Lt. Col. Thomas L. Hayes took the 357th Fighter Group's P-51s on an escort mission to Pirna on April 19, 1945, and returned to hide in the sun over Ruzyne airdrome at Prague, Czechoslovakia. After playing the cat-and-mouse game in the clouds for a few minutes, Me 262s were seen to begin taking off two by two. The bounce was made after sixteen of the jets had become airborne. In the ensuing combat, four of the 262s were destroyed and three damaged.

Lieutenant Colonel Hayes got strikes on the 262 leader who turned left, hit the deck at full power and crossed the river at the southern outskirts of Prague. Here Hayes encountered intense and accurate flak from the ground. Still hanging on, the Mustang pilot lost the jet temporarily behind a tall building on the eastern shore of the river, and as he pulled up over the building, he saw the 262 hit the ground in a sharp turn to the right and slide into a building.

Perhaps one of the most frustrating combats by a Mustang pilot with one of the Me 262s was experienced by Lt. Theodore W. Sedvert of the Ninth Air Force's 354th Group. On March 2, 1945, Sedvert observed a 262 drop a bomb on Osthofen, and holding altitude advantage, he dove down to do away with the intruder. Good strikes were obtained in the tail and fuselage of the Messerschmitt. As it attempted to flee, it began to lose power and slow up. Sedvert pulled in, fired the rest of his ammunition and the jet still flew along. With no more rounds for his guns, the P-51 pilot pulled up alongside the 262 and peered across the way into the cockpit of his opponent. To add insult to injury the German pilot had the gall to thumb his nose at him.

Sedvert figured that was the limit to the whole thing. He pulled his .45-caliber pistol from its holster and blazed away. Still no visible effect! However, as he continued to fly along, the 262 began to smoke and he watched the pilot belly it in near Wiesthal.

Late in 1944 another German jet made its appearance. This was the Arado 234 twin-jet reconnaissance bomber. However, it tended to make only brief hit-and-run strikes and proved to be no match at all for the Mustangs which got it in its sights. The first of this type to fall victim to a P-51 was caught and shot down on December 31, 1944, by Lt. Col. John C. Meyer of the 352nd Fighter Group.

Few piston-driven German fighters were to be seen in the skies by March and April of 1945. All priority had been given the Me 262 jets and several new groups of these fighters had been formed. In January of 1945 the most elite unit the Luftwaffe had ever known was organized under the command of Gen. Adolf Galland. Ten of the pilots in Jagdverband 44 were holders of the coveted Knights Cross and most were high-scoring aces who had seen years of combat flying.

Even this did not deter the success of the American P-51s in racking up victories. On the tenth of April the American bombers were violently opposed over Germany by the jets who took a toll of ten of the four-engined craft. However, they lost twenty of their own number, eighteen of them falling to the guns of Mustangs. In one of the combats, a 262 made a rare head-on pass at the P-51 flown by Capt. Gordon Compton of the 353rd Group. Compton gave him a short burst and the Me 262 burst into flames. The pilot bailed out and cleared the plane, but his parachute never opened.

The German jets and the Mustangs continued to mix it up until the very end of the war, but the Luftwaffe's new planes had come along in too little quantity and too late to do the damage that they were capable of doing. Formations of P-51s over the jet air bases had made operations extremely hazardous for the German pilots and even the presence of FW 190s as takeoff and landing cover was in vain.

The Mustangs from North American may have been outclassed by speed, but when it came to maneuverability and tactics, the steed came through with flying colors.

CHAPTER **6**

RAF AND FRENCH MUSTANGS

MUSTANG Is and IAs continued to see service with the RAF in 1944, but in decreasing numbers. Several of the squadrons converted to later models of Spitfires and Hurricanes, but six remaining units kept their Mustangs on after D-day. No. 2 Squadron became the first unit in western Europe to receive the newer Mark IIs which they took to France in July for operations with the Second Tactical Air Force.

In the course of its operations with Army co-operation units, pilots flying the Mustang Marks I and IA claimed a total of thirty-three enemy aircraft destroyed. The most successful squadrons were No. 400 RCAF, with eleven victories and No. 414 RCAF, with ten enemy aircraft credits.

Few early Mustangs saw service in the Mediterranean area, but during April 1943, 225 Squadron operating in Tunisia received four F-6B tactical-reconnaissance-version Mustangs from the USAAF which it used in the final stages of the North African campaign.

Mustang III of No. 316 Polish Squadron. Note Polish insignia on nose of the aircraft. (QUELCH *via* GARBETT)

Close-up view of the Malcolm hood which was fitted on many
P-51B and P-51C Mustangs.(POLISH OFFICIAL)

The P-51B and C Mustangs equipped with the Packard-built Merlin
V-1650 engine went into service with the RAF known as Mustang Mark
IIIs. A total of 274 P-51Bs and 636 P-51Cs were delivered to the RAF,
with initial deliveries going to the squadrons of No. 122 Wing based at
Gravesend. Nos. 19, 65 and 122 squadrons received their aircraft during
January and February 1944.

The British pilots were enthusiastic about the Mustang III, especially
its range, but were very disappointed with the side-hinged, integral cockpit
canopy. As quickly as possible this was replaced with a bulged clear blister,
similar to that fitted on the Spitfire and known as the Malcolm hood after
its designer. So successful was this modification that many examples of the
hood were acquired by units of the USAAF in England where they were at
a premium with the pilots.

The new RAF Mustang Wing began operations late in February of
1944, escorting U.S. heavy bombers as well as both U.S. and Royal Air
Force medium bombers. Many fighter sweeps were carried out and it was
on such a mission that the wing's initial aerial combat took place. The
three squadrons were flying the Strasbourg-Nancy area of France when
fourteen enemy fighters were encountered. F/Sgt. B. Vassiliades of No. 19
Squadron latched onto an Me 109 and shot it down while the wing leader,
G. R. A. McG. Johnston and F/0 Mutter of 65 Squadron each accounted
for one. The wing lost one Mustang in the action. The next day four aircraft
of 122 Squadron arrived over an airfield at Dôle/Tavaux, near the Swiss

border, and caught a formation of eight Heinkel He 111 bombers. Six of them fell to the guns of the Mustangs, two by F/Lt. L. A. P. Burra-Robinson.

During March and April of 1944, three more squadrons were equipped with Mustang IIIs, these being Nos. 129, 306 and 315, the latter two being Polish units. These squadrons formed 133 Wing at Coolham under the command of famed Polish fighter ace, W/Cdr. S. F. Skalski. Another Polish squadron, No. 316, was also re-equipped and was based at Coltishall.

Both RAF Mustang wings were very active in June of 1944 giving fighter cover to the Allied beachheads on Normandy, strafing and dive bombing enemy troops and communications. No. 133 Wing was quite successful on June 7 when No. 306 Squadron attacked thirty Me 109s near Beuzeville, shooting down five of them plus three probables for the loss of three of their own. On a later sortie over Dreux, more 109s were encountered, with 306 Squadron claiming six shot down and two probables. No. 315 Squadron tapped four and No. 129 got one at the loss of one.

S/Ldr. E. Horbaczewski had led 315 Squadron on a successful attack against German tanks in the region south of Cherbourg on June 22, when the Mustang piloted by W/O T. Tamowiez was shot down by flak. Horbaczewski saw the Mustang make a forced landing in a marsh and decided to see if he could help out. The Polish ace noticed some Americans preparing an emergency landing site, and though it was far from ready and still quite short, he managed to set his aircraft down on it. Immediately he borrowed a jeep and headed for the marsh.

Horbaczewski had to wade water up to his chest, but he finally managed to get to the crash, extricate the pilot and drag him back to the jeep. When they got back to the landing strip, Tamowiez was told to sit in the seat and his commander crawled in and sat in his lap. Then, despite the condition of the strip, the Polish pilot got airborne and headed back to England.

On the last day of June, W/Cdr. Skalski led a formation of twenty Mustangs to bomb a target northeast of Paris. Just as they were diving to drop their bombs, some sixty-odd Messerschmitt 109s and Focke-Wulfs arrived on the scene, hoping to hit the Poles as they pulled out of their dives. However, the Mustang pilots managed to get rid of their bombs and began to climb to meet the attack head-on. As they did, the German attack broke up and small dogfights took place all over the sky. Skalski pulled in behind two of the German aircraft and gave them a short burst. Instead of breaking in the same direction they broke into each other! There was a tremendous explosion and then a skyful of debris was all that marked the spot where the two had flown.

Early in July of 1944, 133 Wing and No. 316 Squadron were switched from an offensive to a defensive role. They were "loaned" back to Fighter Command to help defend England against the V-1 attacks which were being launched at the rate of over a hundred bombs a day. The wing took up station at the airlanding ground at Brenzett about ten miles south of Ashford in Kent and two miles inland from the coast. No. 316 Squadron was assigned to Friston near Beachy Head.

Because of their longer range and great endurance, the Mustangs were used mainly on the French coast and flew two-hour patrols, while the Spitfires and Tempests flying inland, flew one-hour patrols. These Mustangs were equipped with the Rolls-Royce "66" engine which at 3000 rpm and 68 inches of mercury developed about 1650 horsepower. A special fuel (130 octane) was used along with internal engine adjustments to increase the intake manifold from 66 to 81 inches of mercury. At full throttle the average Mustang so equipped could hold about 420 mph at 2000 feet. The average speed of the first hundred V-1s shot down by the wing was 370 mph. The Mustangs performed quite well for this duty, the only difficulty experienced being caused by the experimental fuel that they were using.

No. 133 Wing was credited with downing 190 V-1s during its defensive tour, but there were times when unusual problems were encountered. Such an event took place during the first "doodlebug" patrol of a young Canadian pilot named Fred Holmes. "There was a shortage of fighters that day, so single aircraft were placed on patrols usually covered by pairs of aircraft," recalls Holmes. "The ceiling was low, with rain, and doodlebugs came over steadily all day. I found myself patrolling from Beachy Head to a point east of Hastings alone and was given a V-1 to find at an altitude of 2000 feet, but this was 300 feet above the broken cloud base.

"I was lucky enough to find myself just behind and below this bird over the sea, and between clouds for long enough to fire and see strikes on it before it bobbed into the clouds again. I dropped below cloud and waited for it to come out, but noticed that I was then right over the sea-front promenade of the city of Hastings—and the V-1 came out of the clouds, too. It was losing height and flying under control but obviously damaged.

"A few seconds before, I had wanted nothing so much as to shoot it down, now I wanted it to stay up and fly on and I sat just below it, throttling back, trying to reduce speed and get behind it, but it was losing power and slowing down as much as I was. As it got lower it squeezed me between itself and the rooftops. When the ground dropped away as we crossed a slight ridge, I got out from under and the stupid thing crashed into a field and exploded a block beyond the last row of houses."

Week after dreary week, No. 133 Wing continued to fly patrol against the V-1s. The pilots tired of the monotony of these missions and begged to get back into action in France. In order to boost morale, the wing was allowed to permit each of the squadrons to fly tactical missions over France one day a week in support of the Allied ground troops.

It was on such a mission that No. 315 Squadron gained another great victory on the eighteenth of August, but lost its gallant leader. S/Ldr. Horbaczewski led his unit on an independent fighter sweep over France in the Seine district to see if he couldn't get the Luftwaffe to come up to do battle, and they obliged. The Mustangs made landfall at 9000 feet, flew on to Carmeilles and then to Romilly-sur-Seine where they were to go down and strafe airfields. Near Beauvais some sixty German fighters were sighted in the air and the Poles attacked immediately. In the ensuing melee the Mustangs shot sixteen FW 190s from the skies and only took one loss, but what a loss it was—S/Ldr. Horbaczewski didn't return from the mission. His wingman saw him blast two 190s from the air, but nobody saw the leader get hit or go down.

The Mustang units that remained on the Continent throughout the summer of 1944 gave excellent support to the ground forces in France. Of

A Mustang III with invasion stripes and Malcolm hood. This aircraft of 122 Squadron RAF is in markings of October 1944.
(IPMS—SCHENK *via* ROEMMELE)

French F-6D over the Alps. The French Air Force used these craft for tactical-reconnaissance missions in 1945. (CUNY)

particular note was the work of the RCAF tactical-reconnaissance Mustangs. Flying at altitudes of 200 to 6000 feet, these pilots provided infantry and armored units with excellent vertical and oblique photographs of the terrain and enemy installations. This work was often accomplished in the face of heavy enemy opposition. On July 4, F/O L. F. May and F/O J. L. Roussell, with F/O J. C. Younge flying top cover, were on a reconnaissance mission over Dreux, when they were bounced by twelve FW 190s and Me 109s. May and Roussell became involved in a wild dogfight and Younge dived down into the fray. Younge immediately lined up on an FW 190 and blew it up. The enemy seemed to lose heart in the fight and broke off the engagement. The three Mustangs successfully completed their mission.

By the beginning of December 1944, sufficient new Mustangs were available to equip five more squadrons in England. From these was formed the bomber-escort force of the RAF Bomber Command. Some of these units later received P-51Ds or Mustang IVs, as they were known to the RAF.

An amusing incident of this transition period is told by S/Ldr. F. E. Dymond who was then a young officer just phasing onto Mustangs. "One unusual feature of the Mustang came in ground handling. One had to push the stick fully forward to unlock the tail wheel before executing a sharp turn. This procedure was completely alien to the nature, especially for a Spitfire pilot, because such a movement coupled with a burst of throttle would have smartly had the tail up in the air and probably the machine on its nose! One often saw the 'new boy' struggling to swing his Mustang around in dispersal, one wheel locked, stick hard back and lots of throttle, doing his best to pull the tire off the tail wheel which stubbornly refused to caster."

During this period of late 1944, the first French unit began its transition to Mustangs. In January of 1945, Tactical Reconnaissance Squadron 2/33 of the French Air Force took their F-6Cs and F-6Ds over Germany on photo-mapping missions. The French command wanted to do its own crossing of the Rhine River in its sector, and all reconnaissance of the area from Mayence to Switzerland was done by this unit which was doubly equipped with the F-6s and Lockheed Lightnings. This small unit literally became the "eyes" of the French forces up until the end of the war.

Once the RAF Mustang escorting force got into action in the spring of 1945, they, too, began to encounter the German jets on their missions. F/O "Slops" Haslop, an Australian flying with 165 Squadron, was one of the few to down a rocket-powered Me 163. This action is vividly described by Fred Holmes who was in the air during this combat.

Late in the war, Mustang IIIs escorted RAF heavy bombers in daylight missions. A 234 Squadron craft is shown off the wing of a bomber. (FARMILOE *via* GARBETT)

"We had half-a-dozen Me 163s hanging around above us over Leipzig on April 10, 1945, on a clear blue day when you could see the snowcapped Alps. One of these craft darted at the bombers, and finding itself being cut off by a section of four Mustangs, rolled over on its back and headed straight down hoping its speed would take it out of danger. F/O Haslop was in one of those four Mustangs, and he didn't take his eyes off that 163, not even for long enough to look at his airspeed indicator. It might have distracted him. He got the diamonds of his gyro gunsight onto the rocket plane and fired once. The 163 pulled up sharply and 'Slops' tried to follow it but blacked out completely and lost consciousness partially until the black turned to gray and he could see again.

"He gulped like mad to ease the pressure pain building up in his ears and turned to his altimeter to figure whether the 8000 feet indicated was 8000 or 28,000—the last figure being where he had started from. The machine felt odd and so did he, so he set course for base, flying no faster than was absolutely necessary.

"What we saw from above as Haslop went down was the 163 pulling out of its dive into about four loops and then spinning off the top of the next one and going down and down until it exploded on the ground. We lost sight of the Mustang and were quick to, inquire back at base as to who had got the 163. Haslop was identified as the culprit, although he

A Mustang Mark IV of 19 Squadron RAF, flown by F/Lt. Joe Doley.
Note markings similar to those used by Eighth Air Force units. (DOLEY)

hadn't been seen since, and almost half an hour after we had landed and
the sky was quiet, we heard another Mustang flying carefully home. It
landed so quietly and gently that we could have bet that the pilot had a
headache—and he had, for when Haslop got out of it and saw how much
higher its wing tips were above the ground than those of its neighbors, he
began to understand that exceeding the aircraft's maximum permitted speed
could be dangerous."

Field engine change underway on Mustang III of 260 Squadron RAF
in Italy during 1944. (PALMER *via* GARBETT)

The RAF Mustangs were in action in western Europe up to the very end. On April 16, 1945, No. 442 and No. 611 squadrons claimed their first Mustang victories when they encountered a bevy of FW 190s while escorting twenty Lancaster bombers to Swinemünde where they sank the German pocket-battleship *Lutzow*. No. 442 Squadron got the last RAF Mustang victories early in May when they destroyed two Junkers Ju 88s.

In March of 1944 the first Mustang IIIs arrived in Italy and were assigned to 260 Squadron. In the Mediterranean Theater the RAF Mustangs were almost exclusively relegated to ground strafing and dive-bombing missions, at which they excelled. A second RAF squadron and No. 3 RAAF Squadron were all operating Mustangs before the end of hostilities. In early 1945 these units got into action using 60-pound-rocket projectiles with which they raised all sorts of havoc with German transport and supplies.

At the end of the war in Europe, the RAF took delivery on 600 Mustang Mark IVs at Dum Dum Airport near Calcutta for use against the Japanese in Burma and beyond. However, these came too late. Some 300 Mustangs had been assembled when the surrender came to the Asiatic Theater. Most regrettably, all of these Mustangs were scrapped shortly after V-J Day.

The Mustang really sold itself to pilots of many nationalities as well as to the Americans. Perhaps one of the greatest tributes to the Mustang was given it by the men of the RAF who had come to love the Spitfire. It is best related by one who flew with the former Spitfire pilots.

"No pilot was ever more loyal to his aircraft than the Spitfire pilot, and no one was surer that he flew the finest aircraft that had ever been built. If anyone was going to find fault with the Mustang, these men would. Apart from some short-lived consternation about a structural weakness revealed by dive-bombing operations a couple of months later, they found no fault. The only machine the Mustang could not outfight was the Spitfire, but it offered many advantages in speed, range, comfort, ground-handling characteristics and stability on instruments that the Spitfire pilot never knew. Rather to their surprise, they liked it."

CHAPTER **7**

MEDITERRANEAN MUSTANGS

I N A sense, the Mustang had been introduced to the Mediterranean Theater of Operations in the late spring of 1943 by the USAAF's 27th and 86th Fighter-Bomber Groups flying the A-36. However, when the new Fifteenth Air Force was activated as the strategic air arm in that theater, two veteran Spitfire units received the first P-51Bs and Cs. Both the 31st and the 52nd fighter groups were transferred to the Fifteenth from the Twelfth Air Force and were equipped with Mustangs in which they would gain their greatest fame on their escort missions with the bombers.

The 31st was the first to see action when they took the bombers to Turnu-Severin, Rumania, on April 17, 1944. They returned an exuberant group of men acclaiming the range and performance of their new craft. Only five days later they really won their Mustang spurs on an escort mission to the Ploesti-Bucharest area in Rumania. While part of the group engaged thirty enemy fighters heading for the bombers, the balance of the P-51s bounced another thirty Luftwaffe craft, getting a real surprise jump on them. In the ensuing air battle the 31st shot down sixteen of the enemy, for a loss of four of their own. When the full total was added, another seven probables and ten damaged were added to the score.

In May of 1944 the 52nd Group got in action with the P-51 and on the twenty-seventh of that month, a third Mustang unit was added to the roster. The veteran 325th Fighter Group, which was already a charter member of the Fifteenth AF, traded in its P-47s and flew its first mission in the new plane.

To the 325th fell the honor of escorting the B-17s on the first shuttle mission to Russia which was designated "Operation Frantic Joe." A top-secret mission had been slated, and all of the pilots were anxiously anticipating just what kind of show it was going to be.

"The morning of June 2, 1944," relates Col. Chet Sluder, who led the Checkertails, "we got sixty-four P-51s off and met the bombers and escorted them until we were well into Russia. I had been unable to get any decent maps for the trip and was navigating off three sections, each of a different scale and color sceme. I was able to identify the Dneiper River, where I left the bombers and headed for Piryatin. The bombers went on to Poltava and Morgorod.

"The Ukraine was covered by a solid overcast at about 2000 feet, which made navigation a little more difficult, although the visibility was good below the clouds. This part of Russia is flat and featureless, so I had to fly strictly by compass. Piryatin was supposed to have a DF station to help us find the place, but I called several times and never heard a word from them. After holding my course for quite a time I realized that I had passed the field, so we did a 180-degree turn, thinking I would fly back to the Dneiper and follow it back into Kiev. In a few minutes I saw a 2½-ton American truck on the ground and a couple of Russian P-39s and forthwith landed at Piryatin!

"We were given quite a welcome by the American contingent and the Russians. In their debriefing hut, there was a complete selection of the latest air-navigation charts. It's too bad they hadn't been available in Italy."

The 325th flew one mission from Russia. On the morning of June 6,

ndy-stripe" tailed Mustangs of the Italian-based
t Fighter Group in formation. (USAF)

while Allied armies were hitting the beaches in France, their Mustangs escorted B-17s to the airfield at Galatz in Rumania. Sixteen enemy aircraft were encountered and six of these were shot down, with the loss of two American fighter pilots.

After five uneventful days of no further operations, Lt. Gen. Ira Eaker ordered the American planes back to Italy. The Checkertails mixed it up with a bevy of Me 109s on the way home and added three more victories to their banner.

Some fighter aces of the 325th Fighter Group with Russian personnel. American pilots (L. to R.) Lt. C. J. Hoffman, Lt. Col. Sluder, Lt. Wayne Lowry, Capt. Bob Barkey and Capt. Roy Hogg. (BARKEY)

The ex-Spitfire pilots of the 31st and 52nd groups were continuing to enjoy their successful transition. Capt. Jim Brooks recalls some of the events and early combats during this period with the 31st Group.

"We checked ourselves out in the aircraft without any prior knowledge of its capabilities, other than what we could read from the Tech Orders. In other words, we combat tested the P-51 ourselves. Although the Eighth Air Force had been the recipient of these aircraft several months before we received ours, we still had no knowledge of just what the Mustang would do.

"One particular mission stands out in my mind, during the first few hours we had flown the P-51. I was leading an element to Munich, climbing at 25,000 feet when I spotted approximately ten fighter-type enemy aircraft off to my right and high. These aircraft were approaching us and I called to my flight leader to break right, which meant into the oncoming fighters, but he said later that he did not hear me. To make a long story short, I ended up all alone among these aircraft.

"It is also interesting to note that it seemed to be a mixed force; there were FW 190s, Me 109s, a Macchi 202. They had me hopelessly outnumbered. One FW 190 had his gear down, for what reason I don't

*Gear coming up. Laden with drop tanks a Mustang of the
325th Group, Fifteenth Air Force, gets airborne.* (CHECKERTAIL CLAN)

know; however, he did make a head-on pass, firing as he came. He was of little concern to me at the time because the Macchi 202 had latched onto me and wouldn't turn loose. The radius of turn of the Macchi is better than the Mustang and we went around about three turns in a lufbery circle. I knew that the fourth or fifth turn he would be able to pull his nose around and be in a position to fire, so I split-essed and fortunately he did not follow.

"Believe it or not, I climbed back up again and got back into the fight I had just left. However, I didn't stay around too long. At this time I figured that I had pretty well had it, so I headed for Switzerland hoping that if they did shoot me down I would be in Swiss territory and be interned. Fortunately,

Loading ammo is an armorer of the 332nd "Red Tailed" Fighter Group of the Italian-based Fifteenth Air Force. (WEATHERILL)

they soon gave up the chase and I returned to my base a very frightened, but a much wiser combat pilot. At this time I had only about ten missions."

Since being equipped with the Mustang, the 52nd, a former Spitfire group, had been getting appreciable scores on each mission on which enemy aircraft were encountered. On their mission to Munich on June 9, they found the bomber formations scattered and under heavy attack. Flying into the opposition, the yellow-tailed P-51s broke up the enemy concentrations and proceeded to blast fourteen of them out of the air.

By June 23, the 52nd Group had set a Fifteenth AF record by downing 102 enemy aircraft in a period of thirty-five days. The 52nd's losses were under 5 per cent of the destruction that had been inflicted on the enemy.

Late in June the all-Negro 332nd Fighter Group gave up their P-47s and converted to the Mustang. With their transition, the Fifteenth AF now possessed four P-51 groups that in conjunction with the P-38 units would escort the bombers until the end of the war.

One of the outstanding young pilots of the 52nd Group was Capt. J. S. "Sully" Varnell. While escorting the heavies to Ploesti on July 9, Varnell and his top cover formation sighted some fifty Me 109s starting to dive on the bombers. "Sully" went down to the attack and shot down the tail-end

Charlie of the 109 formation. Reefing around, he sighted another 109 and chased him right in over the target area and flamed him in the midst of flak and falling bombs.

Varnell made a fast 180-degree turn to get out of the target area and sighted another 109. After his first pass, the German plane began to smoke and stream glycol, but he continued to fly. Varnell pulled around in a tight circle and came in again. A short burst right up the rear of the Messerschmitt and the German plane went down for good. "I'm getting 100 per cent on these claims," said Varnell in his debriefing. "I saw all three of them crash."

Another 52nd pilot who had a big day in July was Lt. Calvin D. Allen, Jr. who celebrated a real American-type Fourth. Leading an attack on a large formation of Me 109s that day, he tacked in on old tail-end Charlie and got him with his first burst. Still in a dive, he slid behind victim number two, tapped him and then got a third before he had to pull out. As he zoomed up, the belly of a fourth Messerschmitt crossed his sights, so Allen raked him from stem to stern and down he went. Four on the Fourth is good in any pilot's book.

One malfunction that the Mustangs had been experiencing was rectified to the satisfaction of many pilots during July. There had been some trouble with cooling flap motors malfunctioning which would permit the flaps to go to the full closed position. This caused overheating which brought on engine seizure. Some pilots had managed to literally "pump themselves home" by using the prime switch. One of the crew chiefs of the 325th Group came up with a spring-loaded telescoping rod. If the coolant temperature got too high, the pilot could pull the rod and force the flap open once more. This modification probably saved a number of pilots a long walk home or a stay in a German prison camp.

More confident than ever in the capability of their Mustangs, the pilots of the Fifteenth AF continued to demonstrate their prowess against the Luftwaffe. Three pilots of the 325th sent three Me 109s down over Vienna on the afternoon of July 17 without firing a shot. Lieutenants Stanley L. de Gear, Horace H. Self, Jr. and Edwin R. Williams streaked down on a formation of three Me 109s who were approaching the bombers. "Each of us had a Jerry lined up in our sights," Williams said. "The Messerschmitt in the center spotted us coming in on his tail and in a sudden bit of evasive action, he flipped over and went straight down between the other two. His wing tips struck those planes and all three crashed together. The air was filled with a mass of motors, wings and tails."

On July 22, the 31st Fighter Group went to Russia as part of a task

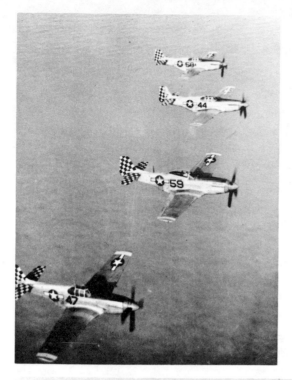

A lone P-51D leads a flight of 325th Group P-51Bs across the Adriatic Sea. (CHECKERTAIL CLAN)

Although "Boss Baby" has had a hard landing, the ground crews were famous for getting craft back into the sky again. (CHECKERTAIL CLAN)

force composed of the P-51 unit and the 82nd Fighter Group in its P-38s. Over Rumania the Mustangs went down on the deck and strafed a number of enemy aircraft on the ground before proceeding to Piryatin.

On the morning of the twenty-fifth of July, thirty-nine P-51s took off from Piryatin to escort a P-38 strafing mission against Mielec airdrome in Poland. The P-38s flew at 2000 to 3000 feet to the target while the Mustangs ranged some 5000 feet above them. The trip was uneventful and the Lightnings conducted a very successful strafing mission.

Once off the target, the P-51s left the P-38s to wind their way home

One of the top Mustang scorers of the Fifteenth Air Force was Maj. Sam Brown of the 31st Fighter Group. (WEATHERILL)

alone. At 1345 hours, the 31st sighted a large formation of German planes cruising along, bomb-laden and headed for an attack on Russian ground forces. There were thirty-six dive bombers, four transports and one reconnaissance plane in the gaggle. The Germans never knew what hit them. The Mustangs dived down and tore the formation to pieces and then proceeded to pick off the singles. When the smoke and din of battle had subsided, there were twenty-seven pyres left burning to attest to the ferocity of the attack. The 31st winged their way home to Russia.

The following day, the 31st escorted the P-38s back to Italy and scored further aerial victories in the Bucharest area in the process. During the course of the Russian shuttle, thirty-seven German planes fell before the guns of the 31st without the loss of a single Mustang.

The Fortresses and Liberators of the Fifteenth Air Force continued to take advantage of the summer skies to carry out their strategic bombing of Germany, central Europe and the Balkans. The P-51s escorting them turned in exceptional feats against Luftwaffe opposition.

The 325th Group was in position over the bombers which were attacking targets in southern Germany on August 3, when some thirty-five enemy fighters were sighted diving on another group of heavy bombers some fifteen miles to the east. Capt. Jack Bond immediately turned and took his squadron to help them out. The Mustangs went into the enemy formation full bore and broke up the attack.

In making his pass on one of the fighters, Bond lost his canopy, which blew off and struck him on the head, momentarily stunning him. Shaking his head and wiping the blood from his face, Bond continued to bore in and shoot the German out of the sky.

August saw the bombing campaign against oil targets reach its climax. While covering the bombers in the Ploesti refinery complex, Lt. Robert Goebel of the 31st Group had quite a harrowing and yet an unusual experience. During the mission of August 18, Goebel found himself alone and on the deck some fifty miles southeast of the target. "Large columns of smoke marked the target area and I was going to take them on my right as I headed for home," Bob related. "I didn't particularly relish the idea of recrossing this area alone and on the deck. My engine was running rough and it looked as though the fuel was going to be close. While I didn't like the low speeds involved in a long climb, I figured I'd be better off at altitude than on the deck. I began my climb and at about 5000 feet made an S turn to make sure I was clear behind and low. I had just rolled back out on course when I heard a bang and felt the aircraft shake.

"I bent it around as hard as I could and then took a look and, sure enough, there were two Me 109s. We went round two or three turns and just as I was closing the gap to where I could get a shot, they rolled out and hit the deck, flying line abreast about 500 yards apart. As I closed on the one on the left, they both started a turn to the left. I wasn't having any of that because it would have put me between them and given the other one a pretty good shot at me. When I rolled out, they regained their original positions. Now I began to wonder how I could break it off without attracting a following. I started to slide over behind the one on the left again, but this time the other turned too quickly and almost passed over me, going 90 degrees to my direction of flight. We were going at full throttle and I knew that by the time he could reverse his turn, he would be pretty far back. I pressed home my attack then.

"Only two guns were firing, which meant that I was just about out of ammo. We came to a slight rise in the ground and he must have looked back at me because he flew right into the ground. Luckily, I was firing at the time and the gun camera made a record of the whole thing.

"The rest of the flight was anti-climactic. I never saw the other 109 again. It was a funny thing, though. When I looked the aircraft over to see where I'd been hit, I could only find a very slight dent along the top of the cowl that didn't look at all like a bullet mark. I have often wondered if the engine detonated from being so hot, just at the right time to make me break."

By the end of August, the great Ploesti oil complex had fallen to the advancing Russians. P-51s of the Fifteenth Air Force now had a chance to assist the Russians by going after the Luftwaffe in their area. On the morning of August 31, forty-eight Mustangs of the 52nd Fighter Group took off from Madna en route to strafe Reghin landing ground in Rumania. Flight over the mountains to the Danube River was at 15,000 feet, after which, two of the squadrons let down gradually to the deck while the third squadron remained at 14,000 feet as high cover.

At 1005 hours the two squadrons of P-51s swept in over the airdrome. They caught the field by surprise and it was loaded with aircraft. Back and forth they screamed like a swarm of angry hornets cutting a reaper's swath across the landing ground. Some of the pilots made as many as twelve individual passes before they broke off and headed for home. When the 52nd gathered its forces and set course for Italy, sixty Luftwaffe aircraft lay destroyed on the ground. Four Mustangs didn't get back to Madna.

One of the few enemy planes that could give the Mustang a real battle over Europe was the Italian Macchi 202. Although Italy had long since surrendered, there was a group of Italians that continued to fight on with the Luftwaffe nearly until the end of the war. It was one of the Macchi 202s that fell victim to the leading ace of the Fifteenth AF, Lt. John J. Voll on September 23.

"On our way home," Voll reported, "I saw a Macchi 202 through a break in the clouds and went after him. Going in and out of the clouds, as we were, I was chasing his vapor trails rather than actually seeing him all the time, and then when I finally got into position to fire, I glanced behind me and there was another Macchi on my tail.

"I started firing, and although I only used up twenty rounds per gun on the Macchi in front of me, it seemed as though I'd used up a hundred before my shots blew the cockpit apart and the pilot bailed out. I started to attack the other plane, but by this time another had joined the fight, and since the Macchi can turn a shade sharper than a Mustang, they soon had boxed me in. I got into a cloud and headed for home."

Another pilot who was lucky to get home late in October was Capt. Armour McDaniel of the 332nd Fighter Group. The unit was strafing oil barges in the vicinity of Odestal when the bullets from Lt. Robert Friend's P-51 ignited the oil on one of the barges and the Mustang pilot was forced to fly through the flames. Luckily he came out without damage.

It was then McDaniel's turn to go down and he hit another barge that set off a tremendous explosion. The force was so great that it ripped the

"American Beauty," the Mustang of the Fifteenth Air Force top ace, Capt. J. J. Voll of the 31st Fighter Group. (USAF)

guns out of his wings. Nursing the sturdy craft home from the target, he managed to keep it aloft until he reached Naples.

With the advent of fall, poor weather conditions not only held the bombers on the ground, but when they did fly a mission, the Luftwaffe was reluctant to combat both them and the massive cloud formations. However, the 31st Group got into a mass of German fighters when they escorted the B-17s to Brux on October 16. Maj. George T. Buck was leading the squadron assigned to pick up the third group of B-17s. On arrival over Brux, there were no bombers to be found, so Buck swung his fighters in a 180-degree turn and proceeded to retrace the route. After only a few minutes flight, a swarm of Me 109s was sighted flying in the vapor trails of a group of Fortresses, closing for an attack.

"We got a good bounce on them, so we attacked," stated Buck. "The flight lasted about eight to ten minutes and the squadron accounted for ten to twelve kills and about a dozen damaged. I got three and on the last one I was in prop wash and was flipped on my back. When I righted the P-51, I lined up on another 109, pulled my trigger and got one pop from one gun. I thought I was out of ammo, but found later my guns had jammed. The final estimate, after viewing all the film, was that there were 112 Me 109s in the formation. They never caught the B-17s."

On the afternoon of December 22, Lt. Eugene P. McGlauflin and

Winter came to Italy and brought snow and freezing temperatures, but the work of the ground crews went on. (CHECKERTAIL CLAN)

F/O Roy L. Scales teamed up to destroy the first Me 262 to be credited to a Mediterranean unit. The pilots from the 31st Group were flying some fifteen miles northwest of Passau near the Austrian-German frontier when McGlauflin sighted the jet.

"I probably saw the jet before any of the others," said McGlauflin. "All of a sudden, I looked up and almost right in front of me was this stranger. I called over the radio, 'George, is that you?' 'Hell, no,' was the answer and then someone squealed, 'It's a jet-propelled.'"

"I sent the rest of my flight with the reconnaissance plane we were escorting, and with my wingman, Scales, took on the jet job. Neither of us had any idea that we would shoot him down.

"Three times the German dived down and then pulled up in a wide sweeping turn to the left. I was very much surprised to find that my Mustang could gain a little in the dives. After the first time, I took a chance that he would pull left every time he climbed and sure enough he did.

"Every time he started to climb, I would cut inside of him and because my circle was smaller, I could climb with him, so I came quite close— within 800 yards—and each time he crossed my sights, I took a shot. I didn't see any hits, but then, at that distance it's doubtful that I could see hits anyhow."

"I was shooting at him, too," commented Scales. "On his third climb

he started a level turn at 28,000 feet and almost headed into me. I was
only 250 or 300 yards away and shot at him with about 20-degree deflection.
I saw what seemed to be red flashes coming off one nacelle and wing.

"He leveled off for a moment or two and then started a dive. At
about 5000 feet, he leveled off again and smoke, quite a bit of brown smoke,
started coming out. The pilot bailed out. We were diving right on his tail—
I guess we hit 600 mph at times. When I landed, my crew chief remarked
that the paint on my Mustang was wrinkled, which means that the wings
had buckled a little. That dive knocked my oxygen system out, so if he
had gone up again, I wouldn't have been able to follow.

"That certainly was a beautiful-looking plane. Silver and very stream-
lined, with yellow nose, nacelles and tail."

Regardless of the capability of the new jet, the Mustang pilots looked
forward to further encounters with the Me 262. When spring of 1945 arrived
they would get their wish.

However, bad weather and reduction of targets handicapped the pilots
of the Fifteenth AF in early 1945. The onrushing advance of the Russians
had taken out many of their former targets in the Balkans, and it became
more and more difficult for the bombers to find strategic targets.

When pilots went to briefing on the morning of March 24, 1945, they
were elated to learn that they were going to escort the bombers all the way
to Berlin. The 1500-mile round trip was a long and tiring chore, but to fly
to the capital of the Third Reich was a thrill that the pilots from Italy had
never hoped to attain.

Though some of the units met with no enemy opposition, the 31st and
the 332nd groups tangled with some of the German Me 262s. By utilizing
the diving speed and maneuverability of the Mustang to best advantage, the
P-51 pilots were able to emerge victorious. On the mission, five of the eight
victories were credited to the 308th Squadron of the 31st Group. Capt.
William J. Dillard took off after a 262 in a long screaming dive that wound
up on the deck. Strikes were scored on the left engine of the jet which began
to smoke and flame. The pilot flipped over and bailed out.

Col. William A. Daniel fired a long-range burst that sent a jet into a
snap roll and then caused the plane to explode. Lt. William M. Wilder hit
an Me 262 in the engine and it flamed, the pilot going over the side. Once
the Mustangs could get in a good shot, the engines of these early jet craft
were extremely vulnerable and inflammable.

The pilot of the fourth 308th victim went over the side while Capt.
Kenneth T. Smith was still firing, and Lt. Ray Leonard got the fifth by
flaming both of its engines.

Lt. Roscoe C. Brown of the 332nd peeled off to attack the jets and found one on his tail. Feinting first to one side and then breaking to the other, Brown got the 262 to speed by him. The Mustang pilot then closed on the jet and flamed it. The pilot parachuted to safety.

F/O Charles V. Brantley got the second 332nd victory when he followed a 262 into a dive. He registered hits all over the jet and had to pull out. The Messerschmitt continued to dive right on into the ground. The third group victory was scored in a similar manner with Lt. Earl Lane pumping lead into the German jet until it went down trailing black smoke and flame.

As the war in Europe came to a close, enemy aircraft became more and more difficult to find. Lt. Norman Skogstad of the 31st Group managed to find a bevy of FW 190s over the Prostejov, Czechoslovakia airdrome on March 26th.

Sighting six FW 190s taxiing for takeoff, the P-51s circled at about 10,000 feet preparing to attack and then hit the enemy planes when they were barely airborne. Catching his first victim while the FW's wheels were still coming up, Lieutenant Skogstad fired and destroyed him and then destroyed in rapid succession two more in formation with the first. All three burst into flames and crashed. Sighting another Mustang with a 190 on its tail, Skogstad fired a wide-angle deflection shot, hit him and sent him crashing into the ground.

The guns of the Fifteenth AF fighters were fired in anger for the last time on April 29, 1945. Mustangs of the 52nd Group dropped bombs on a highway and enemy convoy in northern Italy, while the P-51s of the Checkertail 325th strafed what targets they were able to find in the Udine area. Twenty P-51s escorted bombers of the 310th Bomb Group to drop leaflets on the third of May to close the books for the Mustangs in the Mediterranean.

In a little over a year since the first Mustang had been delivered to the 31st Fighter Group, P-51s of the Fifteenth Air Force had been credited with the destruction of over 1100 enemy aircraft in the air. The contrails of the escorting Mustangs of the Italian-based fighters had done much to emblazon the bridge of victory over the south of Europe and the Balkans.

CHAPTER **8**

CHINA CHARGERS

T H E Mustang was introduced to Asia in the fall of 1943 with the arrival in India of the 311th Fighter Group under the command of Col. Harry R. Melton, Jr. Its squadrons were equipped with A-36s and P-51As which were initially utilized for ground-support duties.

The first real test of the Allison-powered craft came in November of 1943 when the 530th Squadron was pulled down to Bengal to escort B-24s on a series of missions to Rangoon. For these missions the fighters staged out of Ramu which was still 430 miles from the target. This was extreme range for the early-model Mustangs, even with drop tanks which permitted them very little time over the target area.

The first of the missions was flown on November 25. Bad weather was encountered over the target and the problem was compounded by the appearance of Japanese Zeros which made determined attacks. The Mustangs managed to down one of them but lost two of their own.

Things were worse on the twenty-seventh when the P-51s flew the long route to escort bombers attacking the locomotive works at Insein. Resolute Japanese Zeros came up in droves to intercept and four Mustangs were lost, including the commander of the 311th, Colonel Melton.

Two more missions were flown during these long-range operations, and the 530th found itself greatly depleted with a total of eight aircraft missing, due either to enemy action or lack of fuel. It had been a most disheartening initiation for the Mustang pilots, but the P-51As just didn't have the range or performance and the pilots had run up against some of the best veteran Japanese pilots in all of Asia.

Other Mustangs began to arrive in the theater during this period. The veteran 23rd Fighter Group in China received its first P-51s in November and the 1st Air Commando Group arrived in India equipped with P-51As.

Flying over rugged country are two Mustangs of the 1st Air Commando Group. The setting is Burma. (USAF)

Both units put their craft into action at once, with primary emphasis on bombing and strafing missions.

The Air Commandos' first big assignment came when General Wingate carried out his air invasion of Burma in early March of 1944. One of the more outstanding missions during that time was a strafing attack on the Japanese airfields at Anisakan, Burma, on the eighth of the month. Lt. Col. Grant Mahoney, a veteran of early fighting in the Philippines and Java, led a twenty-one-plane fighter sweep against the target.

Each of the Mustangs carried a large drop tank and a 500-pound bomb. On arrival in the area, Mahoney sent the eight P-51s, which would act as top cover, in first to bomb and strafe the antiaircraft positions. When they had made their runs, he set up his bombing-and-strafing pattern. Screaming down to the attack, the Americans placed their bombs on the

Japanese revetments and fuel dumps. Then Mahoney climbed up and directed the strafing runs. Back and forth like bees after honey, they buzzed until all thirty-five enemy planes on the field had been destroyed.

The top cover Mustangs were kept busy, too. After dropping their bombs and climbing to altitude, Lt. Col. Robert T. Smith sighted fourteen Japanese fighters heading in to attack the strafers. Immediately he led his flight to intercept and even though his guns jammed he continued to turn into the fighters until the attack was broken up.

Capt. Erle Schneider was even more determined. Closing on one of the Japanese fighters, he hit the gun tit until the plane burst into flames. However, in his concentration, Schneider had run in too close. Violently he pulled up, but his wing chopped the tail off the Japanese plane and the P-51 went spinning through the air out of control. This tragic act of the American pilot so demoralized the Japanese that they broke off the combat and scattered.

As time passed and P-51Bs and Ds arrived in the theater, the Mustang pilots began to give the Japanese a drubbing, no matter what type of fighter they encountered. One flight of six Mustangs of the 23rd Fighter Group encountered ten-plus Oscars as they were pulling out of their 350 mph dives on a bombing mission near Tungting Lake on June 18, 1944. By staying close together during the first enemy pass, they were able to protect each other and get far enough away from the Japanese to turn and come back into the fight in a more advantageous position.

Captain Murray, an element leader, pulled up from his bombing run and saw a green Oscar coming down on his flight leader. He had 90-degree deflection shot as the enemy dove but got in an accurate short burst and saw strikes on the engine. The Japanese flipped off to the left and down and the Mustang continued to climb. Captain Murray and his wingman circled wide and climbed into the sun.

Flying at 10,000 feet, Murray sighted eight Oscars in a loose formation some 4000 feet below, circling over the other P-51s and Japanese planes that were locked in combat. Diving on a black Oscar, Murray closed to 1000 yards behind, pulled out and lined up slightly below the bandit. The Japanese apparently never saw the Mustang as it pulled on in to 500 yards before the American opened fire. Flames had begun to stream back from the engine of the Oscar as Murray ducked beneath it and the rest of the formation. Murray and his wingman kept going on their course for home.

Lieutenant Mace was also leading an element when the P-51s were attacked from above. Mace tagged onto an Oscar when they came down and followed him down in his dive. Bucking and buffeting, Mace held his fire until the Oscar began a sharp turn to the left but saw Mace's tracers and began a turn to the right. Just as he was about to pass over the Oscar, Mace pulled his Mustang's nose over sharply and sprayed the Japanese craft which burst into flames.

A second flight of four Mustangs went in to begin a dive-bombing run when they were attacked from above by six Oscars. When the Oscar pilots found they couldn't close on the Mustangs during their dive, the Japanese chandelled up and circled until the P-51s started to climb. Then the Japanese

China-based P-51B of the 23rd Fighter Group comes in from a mission.
(WEATHERILL)

dove again, but the Americans split-essed and hurtled downward leaving the Oscars behind.

Lieutenant Green had dived three times to lose the Japanese craft. This time he circled wide and began climbing, but before he could get more than 1500 feet, he sighted another P-51 half a mile to his left with an Oscar on his tail. Lieutenant Green closed to 300 yards and fired at about 10-degrees deflection as the Oscar went into a shallow turn. The only strike noted was a tracer lodged in the wing, but apparently the pilot had been hit, for the fighter chandelled up, then dropped off and fell into a gradual curve into the ground. The P-51s departed without loss to themselves.

Even the superior maneuverability and diving speed of the Mustang was not infallible. Some of the Japanese pilots were veterans of years of combat and masters at air fighting. One of the more memorable encounters on record of P-51 pilots in China was a fight between four Mustangs and a lone Oscar pilot who was respectfully dubbed "The Coach." This Japanese pilot showed all the ability and character of a storybook flier, engaging four of our best pilots and using the best tactics devised for fighting. The fight was finally broken off after five minutes when the Japanese pilot apparently got tired and went home. This was one Japanese pilot even the Mustangs couldn't get.

The main baiting tactic the Japanese used against the American Mustangs was dropping a decoy several thousand feet below a flight to make himself obvious and look like a juicy target. Attackers would be hit by the remainder of the flight above. It was found, however, that with the superior speed of the P-51 at least one pass could be made at the sitting duck with practical impunity. In some cases, even the speedy Tojo fighter was fooled into allowing more than one pass on this decoy. After one such successful attack on a decoy, the engaging pilots went on record with the following evaluation: "It is perfectly safe to attack a decoy in this fashion, especially if you have two to three thousand feet of available diving space below because the P-51 can accelerate and dive away sufficiently fast to get away from the top cover if given a short lead."

Maneuvering at high speed was also an occasional cause of regret for Japanese pilots. P-51s were able to coax the enemy fighters into a high-speed dogfight and keep up with nearly all the maneuvers. However, it was found that to allow the speed of the Mustang to fall below 350 mph put the American pilot at a decided disadvantage.

There was one incident of an American pilot who found himself at a very poor advantage, to say the least, yet he downed his unwary opponent. This Mustang pilot escorted B-25 bombers to the target where he mixed it up in a dogfight and got hit in the aft end of the fuselage. As the coolant temperature began to climb and vapors filled the cockpit, the pilot headed low over the hills for home. The engine began losing power so the pilot jettisoned the canopy and unfastened his safety belt. Suddenly the engine stopped completely. The American had one foot on the wing and was ready to push off when he saw a Tojo fighter headed directly at him. The pilot squeezed the trigger for one quick burst. With this, the aircraft stalled out, throwing the Mustang pilot against the wing, but somehow he managed to pull his rip cord and drift earthward. Amazed, he saw the Tojo hit the ground and explode during his descent. The American was picked up by Chinese and returned to his base.

The Japanese began a great offensive in China in the summer of 1944 and the Fourteenth Air Force was extremely hard pressed to fly its many ground-support missions. Day after day the fighters and bombers of General Chennault's command ventured out to bomb and strafe the onrushing Japanese ground forces. Enemy fighters attempted to take advantage of the situation by attacking the Mustangs while they made low-level bombing-and-strafing runs.

The P-51s of the 23rd Fighter Group had been bombing and shooting up enemy barges in the Hengyang area on June 29, 1944, when they spotted a four-plane flight of Oscars, two silver and two green at about 10,000 feet, flying good formation. One of the green Oscars immediately began dropping down as a decoy while the three others covered him. Lieutenant Putnam dove on the decoy, making a head-on pass but getting no hits. One of the top cover Oscars dropped on Lieutenant Putnam's tail and Lieutenant Trecartin dropped on this craft and scared him off. Another Oscar came down on Lieutenant Trecartin but fired from out of range, and the Mustang, in a 20-degree dive, pulled away with ease.

By the time the Mustangs had pulled up to about 7000 feet the Oscars were back in their original formation, three above and one below at the same level as the Americans. Lieutenant Putnam proceeded to make a head-on pass on the Oscar decoy. Lieutenant Trecartin stayed out to the left about a half mile at the same altitude and watched. Putnam and the Oscar passed in their attacks and began 180-degree turns in opposite directions. This brought the Oscar into Lieutenant Trecartin's vicinity. Apparently the Japanese pilot didn't see Trecartin, for he cocked up in a vertical bank and must have blacked out for a moment.

Lieutenant Trecartin drove up behind him to 100 yards. The Oscar pilot then had a chance to see the P-51, once when he skidded over appearing to clear his tail, but either did not see the Mustang or took him to be friendly. Just then the P-51 began to fire at the Oscar which either started to flip or turn and was caught by a burst in the cockpit. The Oscar flamed immediately.

The three Oscars above either never saw the fight or chose to ignore it. They made no move to intervene and the P-51s left the area unscathed.

The Japanese continued to advance against an exhausted Chinese Army throughout the summer. The number of ground-support missions flown by the Fourteenth Air Force increased steadily, and at long last the cry for reinforcements began to be heard and new aircraft and pilots were rushed into the theater from the United States.

One of the new leaders who came to China was a thirty-four-year-old veteran pilot who was destined to become the top fighter ace of the CBI. His name was Maj. John C. "Pappy" Herbst and he demonstrated to the younger pilots just how it should be done.

Herbst scored two of his early victories on September 3, 1944, when

Top Mustang ace of the CBI was Lt. Col. John C. "Pappy" Herbst of the 23rd Fighter Group, shown here with his P-51B, "Tommy's Dad." (USAF)

he went to the Tsienshan area to skip-bomb the railway bridge. Shortly after the bombs exploded, Herbst sighted two silver Val dive bombers come out of the clouds. Apparently they were curious as to the rising column of smoke in the target area.

The major maneuvered behind the two Vals as they came down to 2000 feet, and exploded one of them in his first pass. The second one flicked down and it was a chase as the maneuverable little dive bomber tried to make the P-51 spin in. Herbst went to work on him right away, shooting off part of the rudder and chewing up the aft fuselage despite the blazing gun of the rear-seat man. The Val attempted to belly-land in a rice paddy, but nosed over on its back.

Two days later, Herbst got into his fiercest fight while on a routine cross-country to Kweilin to take his P-51C back for modification on the link ejection chute. A build-up of clouds and thundershowers was encountered on the mountaintops west of Kanchow, so he skirted around them to the north to come back south in the Saing River valley.

Just after passing Chaling, Herbst spotted two eight-plane flights of Oscars at 10,000 feet which were apparently flying cover for an unknown number below for he got a glimpse of some of them. Immediately, the major pushed his throttle to the fire wall and gained some altitude in order to sneak in on the last element of the eight-plane flight furthermost to the east. Sunlight reflecting off the silver Mustang undoubtedly alerted the Oscars for they turned into him level.

Herbst flew a head-on pass on the leader of the Japanese formation and saw him start to smoke as he blazed past. However, the Mustang took hits from the Oscar formation which shattered the windshield and gave Herbst a faceful of glass. At this time, the westernmost flight of Oscars was coming in head-on!

Major Herbst concentrated on the leader once more and scored repeated hits before he had to break away. Blinded by blood and with only one gun firing, Herbst was fighting for his life. It now seemed that he was meeting attacks continuously. After one pass the P-51 pilot saw a parachute going down before him, so he knew that he was giving a good account of himself. Finally, the single gun jammed on him. It was now or never, for the Oscars were queuing above him like a bunch of vultures getting ready for the kill. Slamming the stick forward he dived downward. Steadily the needle moved forward on his airspeed indicator as he hurtled earthward. Pulling back at the last possible moment, he broke up and away, hurtling over the landscape. He had lost them in the dive. "Pappy" Herbst headed for home.

The Chinese Army had received reinforcements in the fall of 1944 and the tide of battle began to change. However, this meant no let up in operations for the China Mustangs. They continued to harass the enemy in every way possible. On the morning of December 23, 1944, sixteen P-51s of the 118th Tactical Reconnaissance Squadron under the command of Lt. Col. Edward O. McComas were airborne from their base at Suichwan, China. The mission was to skip-bomb the Wuchang-Hankow ferry terminal. On arrival at the target two flights broke off to go down and bomb and strafe the piers and tracks leading down to them. Both attacks were quite successful and the pier on the Hankow side of the river was left wrecked and burning.

McComas stayed above to lead the flight covering the fighter-bombers, and when their chore was completed, he took his Mustangs down to the deck to do a bit of strafing. A number of aircraft were sighted on the ground at Wuchang airdrome and in the course of several passes, McComas managed to shoot up a Lily and an Oscar quite effectively.

As he pulled up off the field he sighted six Oscars above him. One of the enemy craft tailed him and managed to put some hits into his wing,

*Five Oscar fighters fell
before the guns of
Lt. Col. Edward O. McComas
on the afternoon of
December 23, 1944.* (USAF)

*Unusual personal markings
decorate the P-51D
flown by Lt. Col. McComas
of the 23rd Fighter Group.*
(MCDOWELL)

but McComas dove away and lost him. Climbing to 7000 feet, he sighted another Oscar which he attacked from astern, getting good hits at the wing root. The Japanese pilot jettisoned his canopy and bailed out.

Two more Oscars jumped McComas so he headed southeast toward Kiukiang and managed to get away from them. As he passed over Ehur Tao Kow airfield he saw nine Oscars preparing to take off. He circled the field and made a west-to-east pass on two of the planes just as they cleared the runway on takeoff. He fired into the closest Oscar and it flipped over and crashed into the other and both plowed into the ground just east of the field.

McComas then pulled up behind two other Oscars just after they took off abreast. Closing to within fifty feet of them, he fired a long burst into each. Both were seen to crash east of the airfield.

Four days later "Pappy" Herbst got two of his last victories while leading the first fighter sweep over Canton. South of Canton, Herbst engaged three Oscars which were diving toward some American fighters strafing below. Coming out of the sun and slightly beneath, he closed to within 50 yards on an Oscar which did not burn but rolled over and crashed into the Canton River.

Firing at the other two, which split in different directions, Herbst observed hits and closed on the aircraft which broke to the right. Another burst flamed the Oscar on the wing and around the fuselage. In the meantime, the other Oscar slipped in on Herbst's tail and chased him. Going "balls out," the Mustang managed to get enough distance between him and the enemy to permit a 180-degree reversal. The Oscar didn't go along with the head-on pass and broke, in an attempt to flee, permitting Herbst to get behind him. The P-51 closed the gap and Herbst managed to put some slugs into the Oscar before he got away to the west.

Early 1945 began to see the end of fighter opposition over China. The Mustangs continued to escort the bombers and shoot up the enemy on the ground, but seldom did they encounter the Oscars and Tojos of 1944. From defeat and disappointment in the early Mustang of late 1943, the fighter pilots of the CBI had done on to triumph in the later models of the craft.

CHAPTER **9**

PACIFIC PONIES

IT WAS late in 1944 before the Mustangs made their appearance in the Southwest Pacific. First to arrive were the fighter squadrons of the 3rd Air Commando Group. These units were manned primarily by veterans of the air battle in Europe and perhaps no more experienced fighter organization was ever committed to combat.

Had the Japanese still been giving the Americans a fight for the skies to any extent, they would have been meeting some of the AAF's best opposition, but such was not the case. When the 3rd Air Commandos arrived in the Southwest Pacific, the action had moved far to the north, and it was not until they were finally moved up to the island of Leyte in the Philippines did they see any action. Even then, enemy aircraft were few and far between. The pilots were forced to concentrate on ground-support strikes, and later they took to the air to bomb and strafe what limited opposition still existed on the island of Formosa.

Another unit that added some Mustangs to its force late in 1944 and early 1945 was the 82nd Tac Recon Squadron of the 71st Recon Group. At the time, the unit was based on Mindoro in the Philippine Islands. Most of their work had been photo missions, and to get any aircraft fully fitted for fighting was something new to them.

On the morning of January 11, 1945, two pilots of the 82nd Tactical Reconnaissance Squadron went out to their Mustangs to get ready for what seemed a routine mission. The leader of the two, a slender young captain named William A. Shomo, was dropped off at his aircraft to begin a mission that would bring him undying fame.

The two Mustangs taxied out briskly and took to the skies, climbing on a northerly course that would take them to that portion of the island of Luzon which was still occupied by the Japanese. There, they were to photograph airdromes to ascertain whether or not the enemy was still utilizing them.

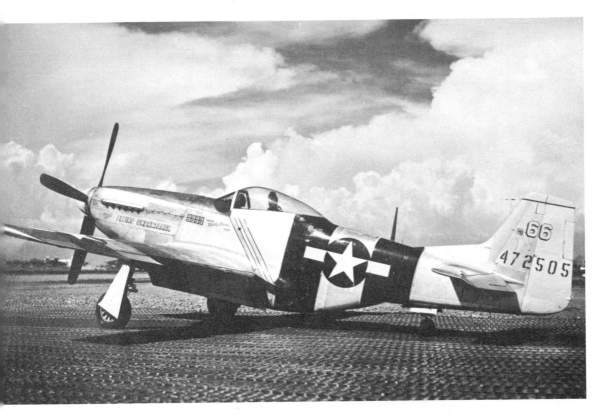

"The Flying Undertaker" was the gaudy marked F-6D flown by Major Shomo. (WINKLE *via* HILL)

Maj. William A. Shomo (Left) winner of the Congressional Medal of Honor for his feat of seven victories in one combat, with crew chief, Ralph Winkle. (WINKLE *via* HILL)

Lt. Paul Lipscomb was tucked in nicely on Shomo's wing as they sped along over the countryside at only 200 feet. Just south of Baguio they sighted a twin-engined Japanese bomber with an escort of twelve Tonys some 2000 feet above them. With an escort like that, there just had to be a VIP aboard.

Up Shomo climbed to the attack, with Lipscomb right on his wing. None of the Tonys broke or maneuvered to intercept during the first pass, so either they didn't see the Mustangs coming, or they mistook them for friendly fighters coming up to join them. Whatever the reason, the two Americans didn't miss. The bomber and one of the fighters fell before the initial onslaught.

With this, the Tonys broke, but seemed confused and befuddled as to what to do. The Mustangs whipped in and out among them, knocking them from the sky, one by one. Nine of the Japanese fighters went crashing to earth before the remaining duo managed to break away and streak for home at full throttle. Shomo had not only done away with the bomber, but had six fighters fall to his flaming fifties! Lipscomb had a real masterpiece to report also. Four Tonys downed in the brief scrap.

For this record feat, Shomo became the second Mustang pilot of World War II to receive the Congressional Medal of Honor. He would score one more victory before war's end to bring his total victories to eight.

The veteran pilots of the 3rd Air Commandos had little chance to score in the air, but did a fine job of ground support during the Philippine campaign. As the fighting in Luzon came to a close, their Mustangs began to fly missions against Japanese bases on Formosa. It was on one of these missions that Capt. Louis E. Curdes had the most unusual experience of his World War II career.

Curdes was no stranger to combat. He had flown P-38s with the 82nd Fighter Group in North Africa and Italy, and had chalked up eight victories in the Mediterranean Theater.

On the morning of February 10, 1945, he and his flight of three were briefed to depart their base at Mangaldan on Luzon and make a fighter reconnaissance sweep to the island of Formosa. From there they would proceed down to the Batan Islands and check out a small dirt strip on one of the islands which the Japanese reportedly were using to shuttle bombing missions against the Manila area.

The flight to Formosa proved to be uneventful, and after an hour of checking enemy activity and weather conditions, the four P-51s turned southeast. En route to the Batan Islands two Japanese Dinah reconnaissance planes were sighted. Swiftly, the Mustangs sped to the attack and Curdes couldn't help but grin when the eager young pilots of his flight sent both of them splashing into the sea in less time than it takes to tell about it.

On arrival over the Batan Islands, Curdes dispatched two of his flight to search the southern half of the islands while he and his wingman took the northern section. Back and forth they flew fruitlessly, when his radio crackled.

"Red Three to Red Leader. We've found an airstrip down here and we're ripping it up. We've flamed three of their planes on the ground, but there are two left."

Quickly Curdes and his wingman banked hard to the south and throttled forward to join in on the fun. About that time a call of distress came from one of the strafing pilots. He had taken a slug in the leg and his plane was badly hit. He would have to bail out. Curdes arrived on the scene just in time to see a parachute settling into the shallow bay off the island.

He sent Red Four scurrying for home to get air-sea rescue out, and dispatched his wingman up to altitude to send out a distress call.

Curdes went down over the treetops and gave the ground installations a good working over with his guns until all was guiet, and then pulled up to survey the situation. From the north a twin-engined aircraft appeared. Apparently it was a C-47, but Curdes couldn't imagine what an American transport would be doing in his area.

Cautiously, he closed on the plane, and there, just as big as could be, was the big white star on the blue background. Pulling in formation with the C-47, Curdes attempted to raise the crew on the radio but could get no reply. Lower and lower the plane descended, undoubtedly intending to land on the Japanese-held strip. In desperation he fired a burst across its nose, but oblivious to even this warning, the transport continued its descent.

Working around to the tail of the C-47, Curdes lowered his flaps and lined up on the port engine. Abruptly he held down on the gun button and watched with satisfaction as his slugs tore into the nacelle. He was rewarded with a stream of smoke from the riddled engine.

As quickly as possible, he slid in behind the starboard engine and repeated his performance. Now the C-47 lost altitude rapidly and the pilot lined up to ditch the aircraft. The plane hit the water, threw geysers into the air and reared to an abrupt stop. Dinghies were inflated, and as Curdes circled, he counted twelve Americans scamper out and splash into them.

Curdes and his wingman continued to circle the dinghies until a relief flight of Mustangs arrived on the scene. They protected the floating survivors until nightfall. It was too late for the PBY flying boat to make the rescue.

P-51D of the VII Fighter Command aloft over the island base of Iwo Jima. (USAF)

VII Fighter Command Mustangs parked in the confusion that was Iwo Jima in 1945. (USAF)

The following morning the PBY went up and picked up the crew of the C-47 plus the medical team, which included two nurses, that it had been transporting. Also rescued was the downed fighter pilot from Curdes' flight. The pilot of the C-47 had become lost and little did he know how close he had come to delivering himself, his crew and the medical team into the hands of the enemy.

For this action, Capt. Louis Curdes was awarded the Distinguished Flying Cross. Undoubtedly the only pilot to receive such an award for shooting down an American aircraft.

In the Southwest Pacific area, American Marines and Army infantrymen had been island hopping. Throughout the summer of 1944, island after island had been invaded and wrestled from the hands of the Japanese. The fall of Saipan and Tinian in the Marianas Islands to U. S. Marines set the stage for air bases to be built that would handle the massive four-engined B-29 bombers. The first Superfortresses began to arrive in October 1944 and the first preliminary missions against the Japanese bastion of Truk were flown on the twenty-sixth of the month.

On the morning of November 24, 1944, the first very long range mission set out for Tokyo. As expected, large formations of enemy fighters were encountered and they extracted their toll of the heavy bombers. This they continued to do on subsequent missions over Japan, but there could be no turning back in the long-range bombing campaign.

It was essential that the B-29s get long-range escort, but it was an impossible 1500 miles from the Marianas to Japan. Not until an island base closer to the Japanese mainland had been taken could fighter escort be provided.

On February 19, 1945, U. S. Marines landed on the island of Iwo Jima. In a tremendous and bloody battle the Marines initially secured enough of the area for a landing strip to be built. On March 6, 1945, the first Mustangs of the 15th Fighter Group landed on the island. Although Iwo Jima was not classified as secure, the pilots of the 15th came in to begin their operations from the South Field strip.

Combat air patrols were started at once. These proved to be uneventful, but the weather was a constant problem during that time. On March 11, the group began flying neutralization missions against the islands of Chichi Jima and Haha Jima. Strikes were flown against the airfield, aircraft and shipping in the area. As a rule, few ships or aircraft were caught in the area, but the bombing and strafing of the airfield went on regardless.

The 15th was joined on the island by the 21st Fighter Group on the twenty-third of March. These two units of the VII Fighter Command teamed

A flight of "Little Friends" escort the B-29s on a mission to Japan.
(USAF)

up to fly the missions in the area that would prove to be such valuable training for the very long range (VLR) missions that began in early April.

The night of March 27 proved to be a grim and gory experience for the officers and men of the VII Fighter Command. In the early hours before dawn, bivouac areas awoke to small-arms fire and insane screams. The Japansee had stealthfully made their way past the Marine perimeter and broken into the camp area. They seemed to be all over the place, firing into tents, slashing into them with samurai swords while laughing, screaming and shouting.

Confusion reigned. Men tumbled from their cots, scrambled for weapons and fired at point-blank range. Many had no weapons and fled for anything that resembled shelter or hiding places. One pilot managed to wrestle a saber away from a Japanese and choked him to death with his bare hands.

P-51Ds with drop tanks flying off the wing of a B-29 during a VLR mission to Japan. (USAF)

With the sounds of gunfire, the Marines rushed into the area with rifles and automatic weapons. Swiftly and efficiently, skirmish lines were formed and a combination of Marines and armed AAF personnel proceeded to clean out the pockets of the enemy. When it was all over, 333 bodies of Japanese troops lay sprawled over the northwest corner of the island. Forty-four officers and men of the VII Fighter Command had given their lives and eighty-eight were wounded.

The big day for the Mustangs arrived on April 7 when they flew their first VLR mission. One hundred and eight P-51s took off from their bases on Iwo Jima and escorted the B-29s of the XXI Bomber Command on an attack against the Nakajima Aircraft Engine Factory at Tokyo. Seventeen of the fighters had to abort on the long 660-mile trek to the Japanese capital, but the balance made rendezvous with the bombers at Kozu.

The Superfortresses were in neat group formations of staggered vees as they headed in for the target. The P-51 units broke out of their loose-squadron formations into flights of four and hastened to get above and to the flanks of their assigned bomber units. These were readily identified by the big, bold and black markings on the tails of the B-29s. Once dispersed, the flights of four began to weave, first one element in front and then the other. This enabled them to not only keep close watch on the bombers, but to protect each other's tail in case enemy fighters dived down from above.

Ten minutes after rendezvous the Mustangs made landfall at altitudes of 17,800 to 20,000 feet, with the bombers at 15,000 feet. The first enemy fighters were encountered over Sagami Bay between Atami and Hiratsuka. Japanese fighters of all types flew to the attack; Nicks, Tonys, Tojos, Irvings and Zekes arrived in profusion. Most of them attempted to dive in on the bomber stream from the front quarter and that's when the P-51s proceeded to go to town.

Maj. Gilmer Snipes was leading a strike of twenty Mustangs of the 45th Squadron, 15th Fighter Group, when the first bogies were encountered. He dropped his wing tanks and suddenly his engine quit for a full two minutes. He lost several thousand feet before he was able to get it started and fly back to the bombers.

An attempted pass on a Tony was unsuccessful, but then Snipes and his wingman sighted two Tojos flying line abreast. As they closed in on the tails of the Tojos and opened fire, Snipes got hits and saw his Tojo begin to smoke. However, as the Mustang overran, the Tojo broke downward and was not seen again. Then another target came into the major's sights and he gave it a burst. One gear came down on the Tojo and then it began to come to pieces. The pilot was seen to bail out some two to three thousand feet below.

In the Tokyo area a twin-engined plane was seen to make a 2 o'clock run on the B-29s and drop a phosphorous bomb. Lt. W. Brown dove down to make a head-on pass and set the craft on fire. It was last seen spiraling downward.

Lt. Charles Heil became a one-man task force that day. Heil missed the three navigational B-29s flying with the Mustangs for the mission and joined three others headed for Nagoya—although this was unknown to him when he tacked on. At the rendezvous he sighted B-29s all over the sky, but no P-51s. Heil continued to fly with the bombers, thinking they were headed for Tokyo.

His engine began to act up as the bombers were turning on the bomb run. He contacted one of the B-29s and informed him that he could not

Mustangs of the 458th Fighter Squadron as seen f
the gunner's blister of a B-29. (US

continue with them. One B-29 dropped its bomb load, turning back with him. Three hours after landing at Iwo, Heil discovered that he had been to Nagoya instead of Tokyo.

The Mustangs shot down twenty-one enemy aircraft from the sky that day and lost but one of their own which exploded over the target area. On return to base, one pilot who was low on fuel bailed out over a rescue destroyer 200 miles north of Iwo and was immediately picked up.

High scorer for the day was Maj. James B. Tapp, who would later become the first ace of the VII Fighter Command Mustangs. He was credited with the destruction of a Tony, an Oscar and a Tojo. He damaged a Nick on his first pass and then caught a Tony in a high-speed climbing turn. As he closed in and fired, hits were registered and the plane caught fire. Then it exploded with one wing ripping away and fluttering down like a falling leaf.

Tapp then observed a B-29 in trouble heading for the coast. An Oscar attempted to get to the cripple, but Tapp cut him off and shot him to pieces in a head-on pass. He and his wingman then pulled in to give the Superfort close protection. This was disputed by four Zekes and two Tojos. The two P-51s barreled in, broke up the attack and Tapp blew the wing off one of the Tojos. The B-29 flew on unmolested.

There was much jubilation among the B-29 crewmen upon their return. Not only had their desire for American revenge against the Japanese fighters been consummated, but they had witnessed the great difference that an escort of Mustangs could make.

The P-51s escorted the bombers again on April 12 and destroyed a further fifteen enemy aircraft and then on the sixteenth of April they flew the first of their fighter strikes which would become more the rule rather than the exception for the balance of their VLR missions. The Mustangs had no trouble getting the B-29s to the targets, but the bombers just weren't getting the desired results from high altitude. Gen. Curtis LeMay decreed that the majority of B-29 missions would take place at night and that they would primarily drop their fire bombs on the Japanese targets from altitudes of from 9000 to 12,000 feet. These missions were so successful that daylight escort missions for the Mustangs were cut drastically. The P-51s were given the task of going after the Japanese airdromes.

The Mustangs fought the Japanese in the air and then shot up planes and installations on the ground. Great use was made of the five-inch rockets which were carried on twin zero-length launching stubs under each wing. These proved to be highly effective against aircraft and other inflammable targets.

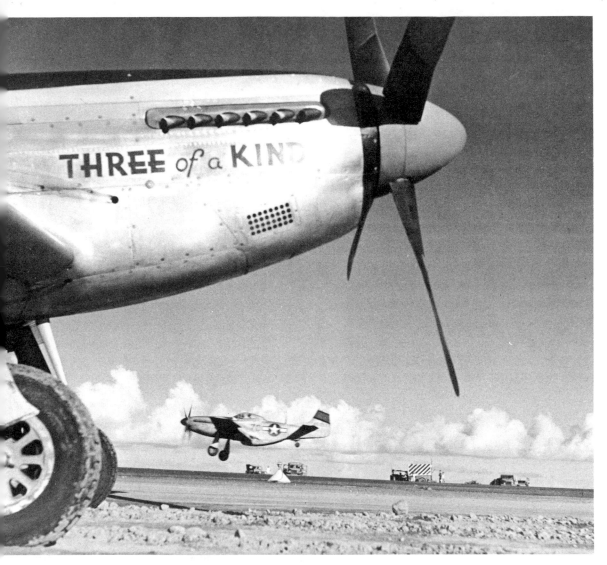

Ready to touch down after the long haul to Japan is a Mustang of the 45th Fighter Squadron. (USAF)

Distance and weather plagued the Mustangs throughout these long-range operations. Jackknifed into the cramped cockpits, the P-51 pilots flew for eight or nine hours over 1300 to 1600 miles to spend a few minutes over the target. "It wasn't so bad after the first hour because your legs got numb," said one pilot. "But when you got home, you didn't feel much like sitting. You were raw."

On each mission, weather reconnaissance B-29s would be sent out ahead of the Mustangs to clear them to the targets. However, the weather on the mission of June 1 brought about the greatest tragedy to a P-51 mission that occurred during World War II.

That day 148 Mustangs of the 506th, 21st and 15th fighter groups were airborne to escort the XXI Bomber Command on a maximum effort against Osaka. When the fighters reached a point approximately two hours away from Iwo Jima, they entered a frontal area extending from the surface to 23,000 feet, where zero visibility, intense turbulence, heavy rain and snow scattered the P-51s so badly that it was impossible to maintain communication contacts. Twenty-seven of the fighters broke out of the front and continued over the target and ninety-four Mustangs returned to base. Twenty-four P-51s never returned from the mission.

In the "whiteout" conditions undoubtedly there were air collisions in addition to some of the planes becoming lost and flying until they ran out of fuel. Two pilots bailed out and were picked up by air-sea rescue vessels. Regardless, it was a sad and dejected group of fighter pilots who returned to Iwo Jima that day.

Air-sea rescue did a tremendous job assisting the Mustang pilots on the VLR missions. Navigational B-29s, Navy destroyers and submarines worked in conjunction along the mission route to pick up any fighter pilots who had to bail out or ditch along the way.

A fighter pilot who would attest to the virtue of ASR quite emphatically was Lt. Frank L. Ayres of the 15th Fighter Group. During the April 7 mission, Frank bailed out 200 miles north of Iwo Jima after nursing his damaged fighter 500 miles away from Japan. He was rescued by a destroyer.

On June 23, over Japan, Lieutenant Ayres was a flight leader of the high cover over the fighter strikes on Shimodate airfield. He knocked down one Jap aircraft which he saw burn and crash and followed a second fighter down to six thousand feet where he lost it in the clouds. His own plane was damaged in an ensuing fight with a Japanese plane which came out of a haze from above and riddled his engine.

Heading away from the target, his plane crippled and his radio out, Ayres picked up a reference point and steered for the area where he knew a lifeguard submarine was stationed. There he bailed out upwind of the sub, rolling the plane over and encountering no trouble getting clear. Remembering the difficulties of his first dip in the sea, he unfastened his chute straps before he hit the water. He landed about 100 yards in front of the submarine and didn't even have time to inflate his life raft before they tossed him a ring buoy and pulled him alongside.

Air-sea rescue services grew steadily during the course of the VLR missions. Before the end of the war as many as fourteen submarines, twenty-one Navy patrol aircraft, nine navigational-and-rescue B-29s and five surface vessels would be spotted along the course of the bombers and fighters on a VLR mission. This service was a great morale booster for the Mustang pilots and certainly inspired them to greater tenacity in their air battles over Japan.

Dogged resistance to the P-51s by the Japanese fighters continued in the Tokyo area. As a result, VLR fighter strikes were increased in an attempt to break the back of this force. The mission of June 23 met with fierce and intense opposition which is best related by the official mission report of the 47th Fighter Squadron, 15th Fighter Group, which caught the brunt of the interception.

"Arrived at DP at 1300 hours and turned to left toward Primary Target which was covered with clouds at 6000 feet. After four minutes of this course the squadron was tapped by seven Franks which made moderately aggressive passes. Lt. Colonel Thomas shot one down as did F/O Jones. After receiving call from 78th Squadron that they were off target, the 47th Squadron went southeast toward Dasumigaura and were tapped by seventeen Franks who came in for aggressive passes with altitude advantage. They made overhead, head-on and high side passes and attacked so suddenly that our pilots had no time to use mutual support and had all they could do to avoid their passes. Lieutenant Ayres and Lieutenant Burnett shot down two Franks and Lieutenant Scamara, Lieutenant Elliott and Lieutenant Baccus damaged four.

"Our flights were pretty well disrupted in the dogfight that lasted about ten minutes. Lieutenant Worton attacked an Oscar from above and saw it hit the ground. Six Georges got on the tail of Lieutenant Scamara and Lieutenant Scanlan. Lieutenant Scamara shot down two and damaged two. Three Hamps attacked Lieutenant Oliver and Lieutenant Burnett who then attempted to chase them, but they split-essed. Three Jacks were encountered by Lieutenant Worton and Captain Martin but they were unable to get any hits.

"A string of Jacks attacked Lieutenant Elliott and he dove to the deck pulling away from them. Lieutenant Elliott estimated that there were twenty-five planes in the string. Lieutenant Scamara and Lieutenant Scanlan were attacked by six Zekes from six o'clock above. Lieutenant Scamara managed to shoot down one Zeke and saw two Zekes on Lieutenant Scanlan's tail scoring hits. Lieutenant Scanlan's ammunition blew up and smoke started coming from his plane. Lieutenant Scamara attempted to help him but was not in position and at the same time was tapped again. Lieutenant

Scanlan pulled away from the Zeros and bailed out. Lieutenant Scamara saw his chute open at about 6000 feet SE of Chost Point over Cheba Peninsula.

"Lieutenant Christian was shot up by a Frank and Lieutenant Baccus led him toward rally point. He bailed out five miles N of the sub and Lieutenant Baccus got Maple Flight to orbit him in the water. He was later picked up by the sub."

The Japanese had proved that they weren't out of fighters and experienced fighter pilots, but the Mustangs had shown that they could take on anything they had to offer and still outperform and extract a telling toll of them.

Two unusual strikes, one in the air and one on the ground, were flown by two Mustang pilots of the 531st Fighter Squadron on July 9, 1945. Captain Mathews, who was carrying a load of five-inch rockets under his wings, was faced by a head-on attack from four Tonys. He fired two rockets at them and missed. He then pulled up into the clouds and came back. He attacked one of the Tonys from the rear with his rockets. One of them hit the tail and went on past the plane, exploding in front of the Tony. The enemy craft was last seen spinning down into the undercast.

The ground attack was unusual in that the P-51 pilot, Lieutenant Thompson, attacked Itami Airfield alone. He had become separated from his wingman in an aerial scrap. Three passes were made. On the first he strafed a George fighter, and on his second pass he flew down to blow another George to pieces with rockets. Two more Georges were destroyed on the third pass by the Mustang pilot who then set course for the rally point.

The VLR missions proceeded to take their toll of Japanese aircraft, and by late July the ratio of aircraft destroyed on the ground began to exceed those destroyed in the air. Although B-29s dropped the first and second atomic bombs on August 6 and August 9, the Mustangs still went back to Japan on the tenth. On this, the final P-51 mission, escort was provided for the B-29s over Tokyo by the 15th and 506th Fighter Groups. Interception was made but six of the enemy were shot down by the pilots of the VII Fighter Command.

On September 2, 1945, Japan surrendered. World War II came to an end. The men of the Mustangs had proven that they could carry the war to the enemy in the Pacific as well as they had done in Europe. Once more they had been victorious over weather, distance, flak and fighters.

CHAPTER 10

POSTWAR

THE success of the P-51Bs and Ds brought many laurels to the North American stables, but there was no letup in development of further models of the Mustang during the war years. The lighter and speedier P-51H took its first flight on February 3, 1945, and showed signs of greatness. Although the new Mustang was some 700 pounds lighter than the P-51D, it had been strengthened structurally and it incorporated a new fuel system which lengthened the range appreciably. It was fitted with the Packard-built V-1650-9 engine which utilized the revolutionary Simmons automatic boost control for constant manifold-pressure maintenance and was equipped for water injection. With the use of the water-injection system it was possible to overboost the engine to develop a minimum of 2000 horsepower for a brief emergency period.

Although several thousand of the aircraft were ordered, multiple cancellations came with peace. Only 550 P-51Hs were built and none of them saw combat. The majority of these fine lightweight Mustangs did service with fighter groups in the United States and Alaska until they were replaced by jet aircraft.

Most fighter units overseas settled down into the doldrums of occupation duty and there was little excitement other than aircraft malfunctions. Such was an experience of Capt. Wendell Hook who flew the A-36 on many dive-bombing missions in the Mediterranean. Hook was operating from Johnson Air Base near Tokyo, flying the P-51K which differed little from the "D" model in that it was manufactured in Dallas and utilized the Aeroproducts propeller instead of the Hamilton Standard.

Hook was to lead a flight of Mustangs back to his home base at Itazuke when he experienced a propeller malfunction immediately after the wheels left the runway. "The prop went into full high pitch as it tried to feather itself," said Hook. "Of course it couldn't quite do that because of the stops.

My wingman went zooming right by me. I had never had a power loss on takeoff, but there was the tachometer dropping rapidly and dragging the manifold pressure down with it.

"But the big V-12 never missed a beat with this terrible abuse (1200 rpm and 35 inches of mercury). I had maybe 50 to 100 feet of altitude, two 75-gallon external tanks nearly full, full internal tanks, guns but no ammo, minimum airspeed. I started a left turn, salvoed the tanks, called the tower for emergency landing, all in less time than it takes to tell.

"As I made the last turn onto a very short final, I could count every pebble in the dry rocky stream bed just off the runway. I nearly waited too long to put the wheels down, but I didn't really care how I landed

"Ah'm Available," a P-51H over the Crazy Mountains, Alaska.
This lightweight Mustang came too late for World War II. (USAF)

The XP-82 "Twin Mustang." This Packard-built Merlin-engined craft was basically two P-51s joined by a center wing section. (USAF)

just so I could walk away. Later it dawned on me that the hydraulic pump was running at half speed or less like everything else. The green light for the gear came only a split second before the wheels touched the runway!"

Although the fervent pitch of war had gone from flying, there were still emergencies such as these for the fighter pilots, and the faithful Mustang with its magnificent Merlin continued to bring them home.

Another latecomer in the Mustang line that would see considerable occupation duty was the P-82 or "Double-bird" as it came to be known to the pilots. In late 1943 it was realized by the design engineers that the extreme range of the Boeing B-29 would extensively tax the capability of the escorting fighter pilots who would cover the long-range missions with them. North American engineers went to work to come up with an aircraft that would not only have long-range capability but also would carry a second pilot who could share the flying duties.

The one and only P-82C. This aircraft was a P-82B modified for all-weather operations. (USAF)

The design basically incorporated two P-51H fuselages which were joined by a constant-chord wing between the two. A rectangular tailplane was used to join the empennage sections, and standard port and starboard wing sections were utilized as the outer wings. The pilot was housed in the port-fuselage cockpit and the copilot in the starboard. This unorthodox craft was powered by two V-1650-23/25 Merlin engines with counter-rotating propellers and each main gear leg was attached to the front spar under the outboard side of each fuselage with wheel retraction coming inward under the fuselage and wing. Six .50-caliber machine guns housed in the center wing section constituted the P-82s primary armament.

Work on the XP-82 began in January 1944, and the first of two prototypes took to the air on April 15, 1945, by which time five hundred of the production model P-82Bs had been ordered. The end of the war on September 2, 1945, brought about the initial cancellation of 480 of these aircraft.

During 1946 the tenth and eleventh P-82Bs were fitted with large radar nacelles mounted under the center section of the wing and became night-fighter test aircraft. Procurement for that year was stepped up for the P-82s and some 250 were built; 100 as long-range escorts and 150 as night fighters to replace the outgoing P-61s. All of these planes were powered

"Ole 97," an F-82E of the 27th Fighter Escort Wing, SAC. This "Twin Mustang" had dual controls and was designed for long-range escort. (GERS)

with the Allison V-1710-143/145 engines, and all night-fighter versions had modified the starboard cockpit for the use of a radar-intercept observer rather than a copilot.

One of the first fighter units ever assigned to the Strategic Air Command was the 27th Fighter Escort Wing which flew the F-82E. (In June 1948, all fighter planes in the U. S. Air Force were officially redesignated with the "F" for fighter prefix rather than the former "P" for pursuit prefix. Thus the P-82 became the F-82 and the P-51 became the F-51.)

F-82Es of the 27th Fighter Escort Wing, SAC, that made the record-breaking Caribbean round-robin flight. (GERS)

This unit made many long-range flights in the late 1940s, the most memorable being an over water celestial navigation operation. Forty-four of the Twin Mustangs made a round-robin flight from Kearney AFB, Nebraska, to MacDill AFB, Florida, then on to Puerto Rico, Panama, Jamaica, Fort Worth, Texas, and back to Kearney. Longest hop was the 1600-mile jump between Jamaica and Fort Worth, Texas, with 1350 miles of it over water. For the conventional fighter planes of the day, this was quite a feat.

One of the squadrons flying F-82Es on night-fighter duty was the 449th based at Adak in the Aleutian Islands. If ever a climate could bring out the worst in an airplane, it was there. However, for the most part the F-82s performed their job well. There were a few hairy moments, experienced when the only instrument inverter, which furnished electrical power for the flight instruments, went out. The aircraft, when first received, had all electrical instruments, and when the inverter failed, the pilot had to come in by the seat of his pants. A second inverter later took care of this problem.

At the end of the war many Mustangs were declared surplus and sold on the civilian market. These craft were modified in every manner imaginable and all sorts of record feats were sought in them, but the main event that caught the public's eye during the early postwar years was the performance of the Mustang in the revival of the famed Bendix Trophy Race. These California to Cleveland dashes were the highlight of distance racing in the 1930s, and the entry of World War II fighters into the field in 1946 was a natural.

As the starting date of August 30, 1946, approached, the veteran pilots worked feverishly to get the fighters ready for the flight. P-38 Lightnings dominated the entry list with ten twin-boomed contestants. Other slated starters were two Bell P-63 Kingcobras, one Goodyear FG-1 Corsair, one Douglas A-26 and four P-51 Mustangs. Highlighting the Mustang entries was a shiny brand-new craft which famed aviatrix Jackie Cochran had just received from the factory and two Mustangs selected from a mass purchase by veteran stunt and movie pilot, Paul Mantz.

A primary consideration of all pilots in the race was fuel load for the distance, at an airspeed which would enable them to win. Permission had been granted to jettison drop tanks, but it had to be done over open country where no damage could be incurred. All of the flyers had been warned that any violation of this ruling would cost them their license. This stiff penalty cost several pilots considerable time in the Bendix Trophy races.

One of the first to experience drop-tank trouble was Jackie Cochran. When she attempted to jettison her oversize tanks, the front ends dropped and the rear held. This caused the nose of the tanks to drop down and kick the rear ends up into the trailing edges of the wings. Considerable damage was done before she finally got rid of them. Regardless of her difficulties she was still able to blaze into Cleveland in 4 hours and 52 minutes to win second place in the Bendix Race.

The 1946 race was copped by veteran Paul Mantz in his blood-red Mustang "Blaze of Noon." Paul amazed the aviation world by removing the wing tanks from his airplane, sealing the wings up and filling them completely with fuel. This sans drop-tank configuration enabled him to cross the finish line in 4 hours, 42 minutes and 14 seconds, for top honors and the $10,000 prize money.

Actually all was not that simple for Mantz. When he raised his landing gear after takeoff, the sequence valve malfunctioned and the wheels folded up outside the wheel-well covers. Through some wild maneuvering he was finally able to get the gear down, and on second try the retraction was properly accomplished.

As soon as victory had been achieved, Mantz went to work on his Mustang to ready it for the 1947 competition. Once more the entire entry roster was filled with World War II aircraft and a challenge was hurled at Mantz by oilman Glen McCarthy's P-38 entry, "The Flying Shamrock." Vast sums of money were poured into the twin-engined fighter which was

The famous red Mustang that Paul Mantz flew to victory in the 1945 Bendix Race. (EARL REINERT COLLECTION)

to be piloted by ex-AAF captain, Jack Ruble. The press gave considerable publicity to the personal bet between Mantz and McCarthy as to who would be triumphant in the race to Cleveland.

However, on the day of the race, "Dame Fortune" refused to shine on the P-38. Ruble experienced trouble from the beginning. He lost one of his drop tanks shortly after takeoff and was forced completely out of competition when one of his turbosuperchargers blew up on him over Arizona.

The real race developed between Mantz and another Mustang; "Magic Town" flown by Joe De Bona. Both pilots were airborne without mishap and poured on the coal in the race of their lives. Mantz thundered out of the west and set his Mustang down in the record time of 4 hours, 26 minutes and 57.4 seconds.

Mantz settled down to await the arrival of De Bona. His wait was short and an excited roar came from the crowd as the Mustang streaked across the finish line. Now it was all up to the timers. When the result was handed down, De Bona clocked in at 4 hours, 28 minutes, 15 seconds. He had lost by only one minute, 17.6 seconds. For Mantz, it was another brilliant victory. For De Bona, a heartbreaking loss with only 1948 to look forward to. For the Mustang, it was another superb accomplishment; the speedy little fighter took all the first six places.

Paul Mantz repeated his win for the third time in 1948. For Joe De

The P-51D that Joe De Bona flew to win second place in the 1947 Bendix Race. (EARL REINERT COLLECTION)

Bona, it was another excruciating loss for he had the race won up until the final few minutes. With the airfield in sight, his engine quit. He had figured his fuel too closely. In utter frustration he set the Mustang down in a cornfield only twenty miles from victory.

After three record-breaking wins, Paul Mantz chose not to enter the Bendix Race in 1949, but did enter two of his Mustangs which were flown by Harman "Fish" Salmon and Stan Reaver. However, this time Joe De Bona was not to be denied. Streaking cross country at high altitude he crossed the finish line in only 4 hours, 16 minutes, 17.5 seconds for an average of 470 miles per hour. Stan Reaver took second place and Salmon third. It was another clean sweep for the Mustangs.

Accomplishment for the Mustang just seemed to keep growing during the five years after the war. Perhaps its zenith for these years was its Bendix Trophy triumphs, but many other records were being set by pilots in civilian status. One of the foremost was a speed record set by Jackie Cochran on December 12, 1947. Flying over a three-kilometer course, she clocked 412.002 miles per hour, a record which still stands for women in propeller-driven aircraft.

After less than five years of peace, world events took a sudden turn that thrust the United States into another conflict. It was time for the little record-breaking steed to step out of the winners' circle and its laudatory garlands and get back into warpaint.

CHAPTER **11**

KOREA

IN THE wee hours of predawn on June 25, 1950, the North Korean Army launched an offensive into the Republic of South Korea. Sporadic incidents had been taking place on the border at the 38th Parallel for some months, and initially there was doubt as to whether this was another hit-and-run raid or full-scale war. As the morning progressed and intelligence reports began to come in at the capital of Seoul, it was clear that this was no border clash. The North Korean Army was across the parallel and advancing all across the northern border.

U. S. Air Force units in Japan were alerted immediately and in view of the impending hostile environment, it was decided that all American nationals would be evacuated from the Seoul area as quickly as possible. Merchant vessels in the harbor were pressed into evacuation ships while other refugees were sent to Kimpo Airfield in the capital and to a smaller airfield at Suwon, some twenty miles to the south.

From American bases in Japan, the range was extreme for the Lockheed F-80 jets, so yeoman duty fell upon the 68th All-Weather Fighter Squadron based at Itazuke and equipped with North American F-82s. To reinforce these twelve aircraft, a part of the 339th All-Weather Fighter Squadron based at Yokota flew its Twin Mustangs to help out with the evacuation.

On the morning of June 26, relays of F-82s took up station over Inchon harbor to give air cover to the shipping and truck convoys en route to the port. Initial air action took place at 1333 hours when a Communist fighter dived down and bounced two of the Twin Mustangs. The American pilots were in a quandary as to whether they were authorized to fire back; fortunately the enemy craft didn't decide to mix it up and sped off into the distance.

The following day was a different story. Five Yak fighters came in over Kimpo Airfield and were intercepted by five F-82s. In the scrap that followed, the Twin Mustangs scored their only victories of the Korean conflict with Maj. James W. Little and Lts. William G. Hudson and Charles B. Moran each being credited with victories. Later interrogation would bear out the fact that Lieutenant Hudson of the 68th All-Weather Fighter Squadron was the first air victor in Korea.

The F-51 Mustangs got into action on the twenty-ninth. General Mac-Arthur flew to Suwon to get a firsthand view of the fighting, and a flight of F-51s from Itazuke Air Base in Japan was pressed into service to assist in the aerial cover during the conference. As expected, Yak fighters showed up to strafe the aircraft on the field. The Mustangs entered battle with the four Yaks and tapped all of them in a swift, but sharp, fight. Lt. Orrin Fox was credited with two of them.

Contrary to these initial victories, Korea was not to be a war of aerial conflict for the Mustangs. Shortly after the initial action of the F-82s they were tied down to defense duties in Japan, and those American, Australian and later the South African F-51 Mustang units that saw combat were committed to ground-support action. Particularly while the North Korean offensive rolled south, Mustangs were called on to carry the brunt of air-support missions, for the jets just didn't have the range to permit enough loiter time over the targets. Another North American product, the T-6 "Texan" trainer was called on for duty as liaison aircraft between the ground forces and the fighters. The spotting and targeting achievement of these "Mosquito" pilots, as they came to be known, would become legend.

No. 77 RAAF Squadron entered the war on the morning of July 2, 1950, when four Mustangs took off on an early morning mission to escort American C-47s bringing wounded out of Korea. The rendezvous was reached successfully and the fighters continued to orbit for several minutes, but the transports never made an appearance. Disappointed and disgruntled, the Australian pilots returned to their base at Iwakuni, Japan. Later in the day they participated in two bomber-escort missions over Korea.

The month of July saw the South Koreans and one American division continue to reel back before the onslaught of the Communists from the north. American reinforcements were rushed in from Japan, but months of occupation duty showed its effect in their lack of combat readiness. However, the North Koreans had failed in one respect; their little piston-driven air force was no match for the Americans. Jets and Mustangs of the U. S. Air Force swept them from the skies and strafed their remaining aircraft in the first few days of warfare. There was no air cover for their troops and they suffered accordingly.

*Korean sunrise. F-51D taxies out for a mission as dawn breaks
over the mountains.* (HOWARD)

Typical of the ground-support missions flown in those trying days was
a strike flown on July 14 by No. 77 RAAF Squadron. Four Mustangs
contacted the spotter aircraft and were instructed to attack a bridge across
the Kum River near Kongju. This they hit with rockets and then they pulled
back up to see targets of opportunity. As they orbited, they were called back
to the river to attack enemy troops who were making a crossing in boats.

The Mustangs roared across the scene skimming the earth with machine
guns blazing. The Koreans, caught in the open, were cut down like wheat.
A number of the troops were caught on one side of the river where they
waited to cross. Tenaciously they hugged the ground while their comrades
were shot down, and, in all probability, they would have been considered
dead and left lying had they not jumped up and run when the Mustangs
came in for another pass. As it was, many were killed as they scattered in
all directions. Then the Mustangs returned and finished off the troops that
were swimming in the river. It was a real massacre.

In order to build up ground-strafing forces, the United States rushed
the aircraft carrier USS *Boxer* to Japan with a load of 145 F-51s. They made
the crossing in a record-breaking eight days and the planes were quickly
assembled and flown out to combat units.

One of the units so equipped was the 18th Fighter-Bomber Wing which
gave up its F-80 jets for Mustangs. This necessitated complete transition

and ground-support training that was carried out on a crash basis. By August they were operating their F-51s in support of the Allied ground forces.

On August 5, 1950, Maj. Louis J. Sebille took off on a mission with the 67th Squadron of the 18th Fighter-Bomber Wing against enemy artillery and troops hidden along the banks of a river near Hamchang. Flying his wing was Capt. Charles R. Morehouse, who was on his first combat mission over Korea, flying a Mustang loaded with two 500-pound bombs, six rockets and a full load of .50-caliber ammunition. In the initial bombing attack, Sebille was unable to get rid of one of his bombs, so he racked the plane around and headed back in to make a strafing pass with his flight.

Antiaircraft and small-arms fire was coming up fast and furious that day. Morehouse said later, "They didn't know that they couldn't get away with moving in the daytime and consequently had everything out to throw at us."

Morehouse's radio contact was garbled. He couldn't make out what his flight leader was saying, but he did hear his element leader, Sebille say, "I'm hit. I'll never make it back. I'm going to get those . . ."

Morehouse followed his leader down on a straight-in strafing run. Sebille

Shark-toothed F-51D is preflighted for a mission over Korea. (HOWARD)

was diving for two half-tracks practically hidden in the trees. Morehouse saw the crash, a sheet of flame and the wreckage strewn over the countryside. Maj. Louis Sebille knew that he had been wounded—probably mortally—and had chosen to dive his stricken aircraft into the midst of the enemy. For this act of final, selfless devotion to duty Major Sebille was awarded the Congressional Medal of Honor. This would be the last such award for a gallant Mustang pilot.

The ground-support job by the Mustangs in those days of doubt and anguish was tremendous. By late August, United Nations troops were strong enough to counterattack and retake some of the ground which they had relinquished. At that time ground troops got a firsthand knowledge of the wrath that had been wrought by the F-51s. In the Kigye area, South Korean troops counted over six hundred enemy soldiers who had been killed by air strikes and a few days later over seven hundred bodies were found in the Pohang area which had been worked over by Mustang bombs and rockets.

Once the United Nations offensive got into gear it was the North Korean Army that retreated under the blows of onrushing ground troops which, in this case, were ably supported in the air as well. By fall of 1950, the enemy had been pushed back far beyond his borders and was reeling toward the Yalu River. It seemed that victory was at hand and there was even talk of American troops going home for Christmas.

United Nations aircraft were overhead everywhere and enemy troops fled in terror. Mustang pilots of the 18th Fighter-Bomber Wing were probably the first to ever take prisoners from the air. On this particular occasion two pilots lined up twelve enemy soldiers and marched them four miles to friendly forces by buzzing over their heads.

F-51s operated in the skies over Korea with seeming immunity until they began to strike the enemy in the vicinity of the Yalu River. On November 7, Mustangs were intercepted by Mig-15 jets on five different occasions. In view of the superior performance of this craft, all the F-51 pilot could do was turn inside of him, hit the deck and run for home.

On November 26 the Chinese Communists entered the war with a full-scale offensive. The suddenness and forcefulness of the attack caught the United Nations troops off balance and once more it was a case of fight and retreat. In foul and freezing weather, the Mustang pilots doggedly flew ground-support missions to cover the escaping infantrymen. On the twenty-eighth of December, Mustangs of the 18th FBW bombed and strafed Chinese troops only 80 yards beyond the lines with such intensity that over one hundred of the soldiers surrendered.

Many strange and even amusing incidents occurred during the many

This Mustang has been foamed down by crash crews after
a Korean belly landing. (HOWARD)

strafing attacks of the F-51s in Korea. A couple of them that were experienced by pilots of the 18th FBW are related here.

One Mustang pilot passed a field full of haystacks. When he returned,
the haystacks had moved to another field. He went down to check them
and started to fly on but suddenly the stacks began to move. They were
camouflaged Red tanks. They didn't move any more after that—they burned!

Another day two pilots fresh out of rockets and napalm saw a Red
tank next to a haystack. They set the haystack afire with .50-caliber machine-
gun fire and then fanned the blaze with their prop wash until the tank caught
fire and exploded.

On the nineteenth of January, the Australian Mustangs flew an outstanding strike on the Chinese headquarters at Pyongyang. No. 77 Squadron
was then attached to the USAF 35th Fighter Wing for operations at K-9
Airfield out of Pusan, Korea. USAF Mustangs had tried for two days to get
through to the target and had been turned back by fog, snow and clouds.
The Australians were more successful. S/Ldr. Cresswell led the first two
flights of six loaded with bombs. After the bombs had been dropped the
second flight of six would come in with napalm while the first six used
rockets and guns to draw the fire away from them.

A tremendous job of ground support in Korea was rendered by No.
Squadron, RAAF, shown here readying for a mission. (USA

Due to weather, the Mustangs got a late start, but at 1300 hours they
swept in and dropped their bombs. Four of them were direct hits and four
were near misses. One 500-pounder was seen to smash right into the middle
of one of the big brick buildings.

Then the napalm carriers came in, and almost at the same time,
USAF B-29s began to release their bombs over the target. The delay in
getting the Mustangs off that day had overlapped into time for the heavies
to make their attack. Undaunted, the Mustangs bored right on in and put
their napalm down on the target despite the rain of bombs from above and

intense antiaircraft fire from below. It seemed that the Mustangs would get away unscathed, but then on the rise from the target, pilot Gordon Harvey called out, "Dropkick Easy One, this engine is losing power."

He managed to put his plane down on the ice and snow on an island several miles from Pyongyang, but rescue efforts were in vain. He became a prisoner of war.

One of the last victories scored by a Mustang pilot took place on February 5, 1951, when a Yak propeller-driven fighter tried to break up a strafing attack. Maj. Arnold J. Mullins was heading a flight of three Mustangs.

"I was just pulling up from a strafing run when I spotted this Yak directly above me. I let loose with a few bursts from my .50 calibers and scored hits on the cockpit and fuselage. The pilot must have been dead because the plane made a sloppy turn and just kept going. When he crashed, it looked like two napalm bombs exploding."

The Mustangs of the 18th FBW took part in an exceptional bombing and strafing mission against Sinuiju airfield on May 9, 1951. In a bold effort the Reds had built new fuel, supply and ammo dumps at the base and had moved in with 38 Yak-9s, IL-10s and LA-5s. The Fifth Air Force

Loaded with bombs and rockets, F-51Ds of the 18th Fighter-Bomber Group head for a ground-support mission over Korea. (USAF)

in conjunction with the 1st Marine Air Wing received the job of knocking it out.

Relays of Sabrejets, Thunderjets and Marine Pantherjets took turns in flying top cover and dispersed the dozen or so Mig-15s which crossed the Yalu to challenge the strike. Waves of Lockheed F-80s went down and suppressed flak with bombs and rockets while Marine Corsairs and Mustangs of the 18th FBW went to work on the dumps and aircraft.

Flashing back and forth, dropping bombs, firing rockets and machine guns, the prop-driven planes worked the field over thoroughly. When the American fighters left the scene, all the Red aircraft were destroyed, a large fuel dump was blazing and extensive damage had been inflicted to every other target on the field.

The last aerial scoring for the F-51 took place on the morning of June 20, 1951, when pilots of the 18th FBW met and fought six Yak-9 fighters over Sinmi Do. Lt. J. G. Harrison got one of them with a fine deflection shot. "Them Yaks are flown by a bunch of Yaks and there ain't no sweat,"

No. 2 Squadron, South African Air Force rocket-ladened Mustang, taxies out for a mission over Korea.

was all that the F-51 pilot had to say about the melee. Later that day a Mustang fell to the guns of a Mig-15, but it was one of the few to do so.

Separate encounters with the Migs took place on June 20 and 28, but in both cases the F-51s were able to outmaneuver the Migs and come home, hedgehopping over the treetops.

Tired, obsolete and weary, Mustangs continued to take the war to the Reds on up into 1953. The 18th Wing flew them until January of that year, and Korean pilots performed yeoman duty in them up to the end of hostilities. This time there was no triumph in a burst of glory. It was not the queen of aerial battle that it had been in World War II. This title had passed on from the Mustang to its younger sister from North American, the F-86 Sabrejet. But then, the Mustang could be very, very proud. As a ground-support craft it had done all that could have been asked of it. It may not have been the triumphant chariot that an aspiring ace may have wanted, but ask the infantryman of Korea about the Mustang. He will always remember it. A lot of Communists didn't live to.

A South Korean Mustang as it is displayed today at Seoul, Korea. (DOERR)

CHAPTER 12

THE MUSTANG TO DATE

WITH the end of hostilities in Korea, it seemed that the end of the road was near for the Mustang. Most of the service's P-51Ds and Ks had been used so extensively in that conflict that they were declared "war weary." The South Korean Air Force took the best of the crop that remained in the theater and continued to fly them for some years.

A few National Guard units in the United States were equipped with Mustangs in the middle 1950s, but all of these were gradually replaced by jets. On January 27, 1957, Maj. James L. Miller, operations officer of the 167th Fighter-Interceptor Squadron of the West Virginia Air National Guard, delivered the last active-duty Mustang to the Air Force Museum at Wright-Patterson AFB, Ohio.

He was met in the air over Patterson Field by Maj. M. E. Nelson who was flying a North American F-100. The scrappy little Mustang and the Super Sabre made several passes over the field for the benefit of photographers, and then on the last fly-by, Major Miller pushed the throttle wide open on the F-51 as did Major Nelson. Of course, the F-100 zoomed up and away from the Mustang in a demonstration of jet power.

The F-51 made one more flight when it was ordered to fly over Marietta, Ohio, on February 14, 1957, to celebrate the première of the movie, *Battle Hymn,* which featured Col. Dean Hess's Air Force career. USAF F-51D, Serial Number 44-74936 then returned to Wright-Patterson AFB to become a museum piece.

About this same time, Mr. David Lindsay, Jr. formed Trans-Florida Aviation in the city of Sarasota, Florida. Lindsay had been an artillery officer in World War II, but had been impressed by the first P-51 that he saw in 1944. He purchased his first Mustang on the surplus market in Canada and taught himself to fly it.

When the Air Force wrote the Mustang completely off its books,

Lindsay purchased nearly a hundred of them, plus spare parts, and crated Packard-built Rolls-Royce engines for them. For the next ten years his firm rebuilt quite a number of these aircraft as plush, two-place executive transports for businessmen and sportsmen who wanted to get places in a hurry.

These sleek ex-fighter planes were sold for less than $40,000 plus the cost of avionics and other optional equipment. This so-called Cavalier version of the Mustang was to gain sufficient attention that in due time Trans-Florida Aviation would adopt the name, Cavalier Aircraft Corporation.

Among the Mustangs that Cavalier has rebuilt and modified is the famous yellow F-51D "N2251D" which was sold to the parent company, North American. This aircraft, flown by the fabulous aerobatic pilot, Bob Hoover, is a familiar sight at air shows and air races over the nation. One of his most appreciative audiences was the American Fighter Aces Association for whom he performed several years ago. An ex-combat fighter pilot himself, Hoover thrilled them with his spectacular antics. One top-scoring ace was heard to say, "If I had been able to fly a Mustang like that, boy, what a score I could have run up!"

A rare photo of a U. S. Army F-51D used as a chase plane at Edwards AFB in 1968. (MERYMAN)

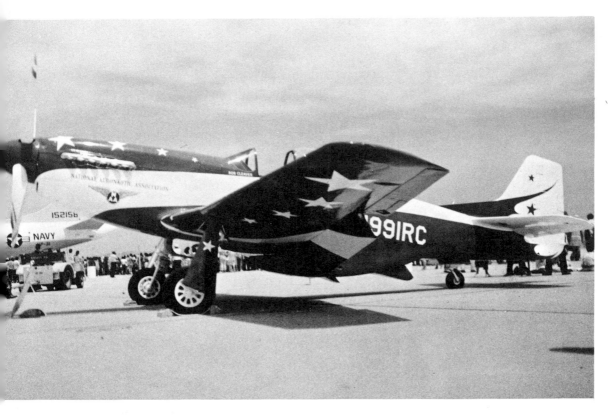

Beautifully painted Mustang belonging to the National Aeronautics Association.
(MERYMAN)

One of the current racing craft undergoing modification at Van Nuys, California.
(MERYMAN)

Other than the brilliantly painted Cavaliers which were occasionally seen in and out of major airports, the public saw little and heard little of the Mustang until big-bore racing was revived in 1964. Transcontinental racing as well as pylon racing has made a comeback, but it seems that the latter attracts the most attention these days.

Racing has brought a new generation of pilots to the forefront of their fields and excellent performances are turned in while flying their World War II vintage aircraft. Of course, with new fuels, additives and material for modification that have come to light, they are able to get more out of their Mustangs than some of the early postwar pilots could have dreamed of.

With their souped-up engines, burning 145-octane fuel and using anti-detonation injection, men like Chuck Lyford, Ed Weiner and Chuck Hall really blaze around the pylons pulling in excess of 100 inches of mercury at times. In recent races Mustangs have averaged better than 388 miles per hour for ten- and twelve-lap pylon races. Pulling those "Gs" around the course and streaking down the straightaways, the Mustang still manages to give a real good account of itself.

Much work and ingenuity go into modifying the modern-day racing Mustang. Most of the craft have the wings clipped up to four feet and have fiberglass tips. Stabilizers have been shortened, and modified propellers and canopies have been installed. Engines are modified to give the greatest possible power for just a short time. This calls for real mechanical engineering and testing right up until racetime. With the margin worked so close for performance, it's not odd that a number of the pilots have had their engines blow up on them during a race.

Bob Hoover is often the starter at the big-bore races. He gets the fighters into starting formation and flies right with them to the starters' point. Then Bob gets overhead and monitors the race. Several tragic accidents have been prevented by his timely commentary and advice to the pilots down below.

If an emergency does occur during the race, all pilots pull up to five hundred feet and give the aircraft in trouble the complete right-of-way. This gives the man in trouble plenty of room to come in dead stick. Then the racers are cleared to drop back down to low altitude and resume their four to five "G" loads around the pylons.

For safety's sake the majority of air racing is now done in Reno or Las Vegas, Nevada, where good airfields are available and there is not a housing congestion below. Through the efforts of these fine pilots and the interest of the public, it would appear that some of the Mustangs are still going to be around on the racing circuit for some years to come.

Cavalier Aircraft's civilian model in the background and Military Assistance Program Mustang I in the foreground. These are modified F-51Ds. (CAVALIER AIRCRAFT)

In 1967, Cavalier Aircraft Corporation received an order for twelve rebuilt Mustangs from the U. S. Air Force. The planes were not slated for use in the United States, but were for the Military Assistance Program. The first of these fighter planes to go to Central America for counter-insurgency work bore full camouflage paint and were as shiny new as the first P-51A that ever headed for combat duty.

Most of the Mustangs being turned out are single-seat fighters, but some of them are two seated to carry an observer. A few models have been turned out with dual controls for training purposes.

The basic fighter plane uses the old standard wings and fuselage, but has a higher vertical stabilizer as did the P-51H. While basic armament consists of the regular six .50-caliber machine guns, the wings have been strengthened and there are four hardpoints under each wing. The inboard hardpoints can carry either a 110-gallon drop tank or one 1000-pound bomb. The other points are designed to carry five-inch rockets.

In late 1967, Cavalier introduced the Mustang II which principally still has the same features as the original Mustang. However, the Mustang II has further increasingly strengthened wings and fuselage, and provides six hardpoints under each wing for ordnance load. Permanent centerline fuel tanks are mounted on the tips of each wing and each will carry 110 gallons of fuel.

With full ordnance load and fuel load, the Mustang II in this new configuration has an endurance of seven and a half hours which would give it an excellent on-station time for counterinsurgency work. Instead of the old V-1650 engine, a 1760 horsepower Merlin 620 is used which increases the gross load capability by some 1200 pounds.

The latest thing from Cavalier is the Mustang III which incorporates a Rolls-Royce Dart turboprop engine, giving the plane a maximum dash speed over the target of approximately 470 knots. Standard armament is six .50-caliber machine guns with provision for six minigun pods to be mounted under the wings. Provision is also provided to carry 110-gallon drop tanks on the two inboard-wing stations for extended range and loiter time.

Mustang III fitted with
Rolls-Royce Dart turboprop
engine is the latest
modification from Florida-
based Cavalier Aircraft.
(CAVALIER AIRCRAFT)

Clean and compact is the
cockpit of the Mustang III
from Cavalier. Armament
switches are on left panel.
(CAVALIER AIRCRAFT)

valier's Mustang II on first
flight. Note tiptanks and
nouflage paint job. This craft
itted for counterinsurgency
rk. (CAVALIER AIRCRAFT)

Regardless of the government decisions on any of these later-type Mustangs, it looks as though Cavalier Aircraft will be at work for quite some time on the versatile little fighters.

It is estimated that there are at least 150 Mustangs flying under civilian registration in the United States at the present time. These coupled with the Mustangs that Cavalier will be turning out for some time assure us that a number of years will pass before one has to go to a museum to see the sleek-lined aircraft. And as long as old fighter pilots gather to put in a little hangar flying time, there are many, many of them who will attest to the fact that "the Mustang was the best fighter plane that ever flew."

APPENDIX

FLYING EVALUATION OF P-51 B AND D

(As given by Lt. Col. Richard E. Turner, member of the 354th Fighter Group, 356th Fighter Squadron which was the first operational fighter unit of WW II to fly the Mustang in combat. Lt. Colonel Turner flew 109 missions for a total of 309 combat hours in the P-51 and is officially credited with eleven aerial victories, two V-1s and has numerous probables and damaged credits in the air.)

I quote a phrase often used by pilots of the Mustang as the most apt comment I know of which demonstrates the true feeling of practically every pilot who had the good fortune to gain proficiency in flying the P-51. This phrase was, "She's as honest as the day is long and she hasn't a mean bone in her beautiful body!"

The wide landing gear span made takeoff and landing a pleasure to perform and the stall characteristics were straightaway, with an ample warning nibble at the stick to tell the pilot, well in advance, of the imminent drop of the left wing as torque snatched at the completely stalled aircraft. Even after experiencing the dropping left wing, one could regain flying control by applying full throttle and co-ordinating right rudder.

Rudder control during taxi operations on the ground was positive, due to a mechanical linkage hookup between the rudder action and the tail wheel when the stick was held to the rear of center position, thus enabling the pilot to steer the aircraft into gradual turns without using the brakes. During ground operation it was SOP [standard operating procedure] to place the coolant flaps in the manual full-open position, returning them to automatic-control operation in the pretakeoff check. Thereafter, the heat requirements of the engine automatically adjusted the coolant flaps.

As a rule, I kept my fighter trimmed for combat-cruise conditions since the majority of my flighttime was under these circumstances. Normally, the only major departure from this trim configuration occurred when I found myself under prolonged instrument conditions, at which time I could trim for the speed and conditions at hand. I found that this practice relieved me from some of the physical strain generated on instruments, and therefore helped reduce somewhat the rate of build-up of mental tension inevitably acquired while endeavoring to penetrate a frontal system, or letting down through huge weather build-ups over home-base area after returning from a combat mission over the Continent. Although the Mustang flew well under instrument conditions, due in my opinion to the light control feel and quick response to any maneuver, I was never loath to grab a free letdown by latching onto a handy bomber formation when I could find one letting down in my vicinity. The bomber boys didn't seem to mind my hitch-hiking tendencies on instruments, in fact several times the bomber that I glued onto would flip on his running lights to help me keep visual contact in the thick weather. It was rather like a case of "You scratch my back and I'll scratch yours." Actually the instrument flying didn't bother me as much as the thought of letting down in the soup amid all the hundreds of other bombers and fighters that had to be doing the same thing in a mad, crazy-quilt pattern of descending aircraft. Tucked into the middle of a nice bunch of B-17s gave me the comforting feeling of having a solid barrier between me and other aircraft in my particular bit of sky.

The general flight characteristics of the Mustang were all that a pilot could ask, especially the original P-51B. As a matter of fact, I felt that the P-51 made most pilots look much better than their level of skill should allow them to appear. It took a pretty heavy-handed man with a proclivity or propensity toward mental lapse in order to actually look bad as a pilot in a Mustang, for the sleek little fighter had a most forgiving nature. In comparison with other fighters in combat of its era, such as the P-47, P-38, P-40, Me 109 and FW 190, the Mustang performed most favorably in practically every category.

Two features of the power plant on the Mustang which pilots enjoyed particularly consisted of the supercharger and fuel-mixture-control arrangement. They were both actuated and controlled by a barometric switch. In the case of the supercharger, your crew chief could preset the altitude at which you wanted the extra boost to cut in and the barometric switch automatically cut in at that altitude without further bother to the pilot. We set ours for 14,000 feet cut in, and there was no doubt in the pilot's mind as to when it cut in, for he felt a definite surge of new power which provided him with a kick in the tail to remind him that he had new horses to chase the enemy. The mixture control when in the auto position likewise had a barometric sensing switch which maintained the correct mixture according to the altitude of the aircraft, and in the heat of combat the less a pilot has to dwell on the operation requirements of his equipment, the better he can concentrate on the tactical problems at hand which could in almost every combat engagement mean the difference between success and disaster.

According to the specifications, the Mustang was supposed to be able to deliver a maximum speed of 395 mph at 5000 feet, but from my personal experience I know this to be a low figure, for I attained maximum speeds of 450 mph straight and level while chasing and catching the notorious "Buzz-bomb" or V-1s as the Germans called them. As far as comparable fighter speeds are concerned, I have only the combat fighter pilot's measuring stick to go by. I remember clearly that I was able to close and catch any bogey within reasonable range that I chased with determination, and due to the ample confidence instilled in me via my faith in the Mustang's capability to take all comers, I did not participate in any combat engagement with the enemy without feeling an underlying conviction that I was the hunter and not the hunted.

One of the many factors which fostered and bolstered this feeling was the excellent maneuvering ability, radius of turn and rate of roll. The P-51 could keep up with any aircraft and surpass most in this department so dear to a fighter-pilot's heart. The P-51B was a veritable dream come true for a pilot in this department. It was the first aircraft that I had ever flown that I could pull up from cruising power to execute a perfect loop without adding power; to me this added up to a near-perfect wedding of power to weight ratio which gave the Mustang its nimbleness in maneuver and delicate but good feel through the control stick.

As usual, when the engineers tried improving the original model with modifications and added features, they increased the weight without a commensurate increase in power; so when the P-51D came out later, it lacked some of the delicate balance and aerobatic capabilities. But with its improved visibility and still good performance, compared to the enemy equipment, it was still a winner. After I flew it a short while I enjoyed and believed in it as much as I had the "B" model.

One of the few disadvantages found in the P-51B was the greenhouse·

type canopy on the production model which severely restricted visibility, especially to the rear, but this was soon remedied by the availability of an English modification known as the Malcolm hood. This modification gave the best visibility that I was ever to enjoy from the cockpit of a fighter. I could actually lean out of the cockpit and look under and behind my own fighter's tail area, a very comforting bit of insurance to have available during a large helter-skelter mixed-up dogfight. The P-51D which followed had a one-piece plastic canopy that approached this visibility, but which did not quite equal it.

An operational bug which developed and gave us temporary trouble was the four .50-caliber machine guns. They were mounted on an angle canted to the inboard around thirty degrees instead of upright, due to the thin profile of the laminar-flow wing design. This angle-off mounting caused a binding effect to be exerted on the ammo belts during turns of any appreciable G-force which in turn tended to cause at least three of the guns to jam. Since the pilot had no clearing mechanism and G-force was almost synonymous with combat for fighters, this problem gave us great concern at first. The only recourse a pilot had, since one firing gun usually rendered using the gunsight useless, was to ride the rudders and spray the bullets from the remaining working gun like a hose, hoping for a lucky hit. Again this deficiency was corrected in short order by a modification figured out and installed by our own ingenious and hard-working ground crewmen. They liberated some ammo-booster motors from a B-26 group nearby and rigged them on our fighter's ammo belts which for all practical purposes eliminated all such stoppages in the future. In the later model P-51D there were six guns, but all were mounted upright, effectively solving the former problem.

While engaging enemy aircraft in aerial combat, I found the P-51B and D equal to all demands and maneuvering requirements that I asked of it. The only area of flying under combat conditions that I consciously avoided was that of a low speed which I felt robbed my Mustang of its intrinsic design advantages. In normal combat speeds between 300 and 420 mph, the controls retained good feel and flexibility which subconsciously prompted good natural co-ordination and flying skill from the pilot while he concentrated wholly upon the tactical situation or requirement at hand. Even in the extreme high speeds attained in vertical dives while chasing a fleeing enemy aircraft, the Mustang was manageable for the pilot who maintained his composure and was responsive to the message relayed through the feel of the controls of the aircraft. From 500 mph through 650 mph in a protracted vertical dive, the controls stiffened appreciably and tended to slip quickly into compression stalls upon direct-manual effort to pull out of the dive by exerting back pressure on the control column. This clumsy manual effort during a high-speed pullout was about the only maneuver where pilot error could materially affect a design overload which could cause airframe damage or destruction in the case of a ham-fisted insensitive pilot. I went through several of these very high-speed dives, and actually experienced compressibility buffeting from a speed which I assume was in excess of the design limit, since I was going straight down at the time, with the airspeed needle quivering against the stop peg past 650 mph. This was before even attempting a pullout. In every instance I effected a controlled pullout by initiating recovery procedure through rudder-tab-control action until the aircraft flew through the critical bottom-out portion of the recovery, at which time normal manual-control characteristics returned almost immediately.

Up until the Mustang arrived on the combat scene in the ETO in November 1943, the favorite effective evasive maneuver of the Me 109s was to roll over on their backs and split-ess in a vertical dive for the deck, relying on their quick-diving acceleration speed to extricate them from trouble. The Mustang literally blew this evasive tactic into the halls of hades. With Mustangs around, the Me 109 pilot could hardly get his plane into the vertical position before he found a couple of P-51s closing into deadly range behind him. From 30,000 feet I could spot an Me 109 a 5000-foot head start in a dive and catch him before he passed 15,000 feet. We considered diving enemy aircraft as easy meat.

High-altitude performance of the Mustang left little to be desired when compared to the capabilities of the enemy. To demonstrate this point I recall one particular escort mission on April 8, 1944, during which we escorted B-17s. The big friends were flying inbound around 25,000 feet, approaching their IP [initial point] deep inside Germany, and our group had its Mustangs deployed around the bomber stream to intercept any enemy fighter thrusts at the bombers. I had two flights of my 356th Fighter Squadron at 27,000 feet just over the bomber stream, on station as high cover. We had been flying our sector patrol for about fifteen minutes after rendezvous when I discovered very high contrails approaching the bomber stream from the interior at extremely high altitude. I was slightly startled at the apparent altitude of the bogies, which I judged to be around 40,000 feet. I disengaged my own Red Flight from area patrol, leaving the other flight to mind the store, and commenced climbing to intercept the contrails which had to be enemy fighters, considering the unfriendly direction from which they were coming.

After ten to fifteen minutes of maximum climbing, we found ourselves converging on a collision course with twenty Me 109s. We had no choice in giving the enemy a height advantage as we closed from below, but I considered this compensated for by the fact we had them in sight and lined up for instant-attack-position pass, if needed, from the start of our intercepting climb. As we were closing into approximate firing range, I noticed the altimeter needle nibbling at 40,000 feet on the dial, but I still had a positive feel and control response with no apparent mushiness or lag time. I picked out the nearest enemy fighter with my gun-sight pip as the German formation tried to roll turn into us for a pass. Instead, almost as if on cue, the whole gaggle of enemy planes stalled and snap-rolled into a gyrating mass of uncontrollable spins in the rarefied air. I saw at least one mid-air collision between three or four Me 109s as the stricken and floundering mass of fighters dropped helplessly below us.

Instantly, on instinct I rolled my own flight into an attack on the mass of milling German fighters presented to us by virtue of the mass error committed before our guns. Those beautiful little Mustangs answered their controls without protest of any sort and we were able to make three deadly passes through the frantic melee of struggling Germans, scoring from four to six kills before they could recover control. It was an awesome but confidence-building experience for us and exposed depths of capability in our Mustangs that we hadn't realized they possessed.

Our Mustangs were the first long-range fighters in the ETO capable of penetrating enemy territory as deeply as the heavy bombers, and although we were assigned administratively to the Ninth Air Force, we were flying operationally under the Eighth Air Force. This unique arrangement was fostered by the fact that we were the only fighters available that could provide escort over targets deep inside Germany as well as penetration and withdrawal. We didn't mind or object to this arrangement because we were afforded ample opportunity to engage and destroy enemy fighters which is the ultimate reward to a fighter pilot. But some months before D-day of the invasion of the Continent, we found our usual heavy-escort missions being interspersed between new tactical support-type missions such as dive bombing, area interdiction strafing and armed reconnaissance which required a superior low-altitude performance from our aircraft. Once again the Mustang displayed an excellent degree of adaptability and a capability to execute the critical maneuvering close to the ground required to successfully carry out these new-type missions. Here again, the P-51B and D by virtue of their maneuvering nimbleness brought new enthusiasm, verve and style to tactical support work.

I agree that the sturdy indefatigable work horse, the P-47, on the face of it, was less vulnerable to ground fire with its huge air-cooled power plant, but at the same time it was much larger and less maneuverable at low altitude. The Mustang on the other hand was a smaller target, requiring less maneuvering room and could get in and out quicker on a strike with better visual coverage. At any rate, all ground tactical targets which possessed any appreciable concentration of ground-defense firepower was more or less like playing Russian roulette to a fighter pilot. He assumed the fatalist's attitude of throw the dice and take your chances! The opportunity and excitement of firing on a target was more than enough to enable the confirmed fighter pilot to forget or dismiss the unfavorable odds attributed to low-level work.

In summation the inevitable conclusion concerning the P-51B and D Mustang fighter of World War II has to be that it is acknowledged as the best all-around fighter aircraft of its era. With pilotage being equal, it could match the performance of any competitor, friend or foe, and more often than not come up with that something extra in performance that enabled it to emerge as top dog in any fight. As dramatic proof of this contention that I can vouch for from personal knowledge, my squadron, the 356th Fighter Squadron of the 354th Fighter Group, flew approximately eighteen months of continuous combat operations during which it participated in every known type of mission. As a result the squadron destroyed over two hundred enemy aircraft in the air and lost only twenty-two pilots as fatal casualties from all causes, training accidents as well as combat losses. This unusual record of kills versus losses was made possible, for the most part, due to the intrinsic advantage afforded us by the superior capabilities of our aircraft, the P-51B and P-51D Mustangs.

TABLE OF MUSTANG VITAL STATISTICS

Model	Engine	Top Speed MPH	Wing Span	Length	Loaded Weight Lbs.	Quan.	Remarks
NA-73X	1100 h.p.-Allison V-1710-39	–	37'	32'3"	7965	1	Original prototype
Mustang I	1100 h.p.-Allison V-1710-39	380	37'	32'3"	8606	320	To Royal Air Force. 4–.30-cal. & 4–.50-cal. machine guns. Serials AG 345/664. 4th and 10th Mustang Is production models to USAAC Serial AC 41–38 & 39.
XP-51	1100 h.p.-Allison V-1710-39	380	37'	32'3"	8606	(2)	
Mustang I	1100 h.p.-Allison V-1710-39	382	37'	32'3"	8625	300	Forward coolant scoop redesigned. Serials AL 958/999, Am 100/257, AP 164/263.
P-51	1100 h.p.-Allison V-1710-39	387	37'	32'3"	8800	148	Originally ordered by Royal Air Force. Armed w/4–20-mm cannon. 93 to Royal Air Force as Mustang IAs and 55 to USAAF as F-6As w/K-24 cameras.
P-51A	1200 h.p.-Allison V-1710-81	390	37'	32'3"	9000	310	Engine change. 4–.50-cal. machine guns. 50 to Royal Air Force as Mustang II.
XP-51B	1360 h.p.-Packard V-1650-3	441	37'	32'3"	8430	(2)	P-51 w/engine change. 1st designated XP-78. Serial 41–37352 & 41–37421.
A-36	1325 h.p.-Allison V-1710-87	356	37'	32'3"	10,000	500	P-51 w/dive flaps and wing racks. Serials 42

Model	Engine					No.	Remarks
P-51B-10-NA	1360 h.p.-Packard V-1650-3	436	37'	32'3"	11,800	1398	Production model w/ Packard-built Merlin engine. 4–.50-cal. machine guns. Serials 42–106429/738, 43–6313/7202, 43–12093/492. 274 P-51Bs to Royal Air Force as Mustang III. 71 P-51Bs modified to F-6C-NA.
P-51B-15-NA	1450 h.p.-Packard V-1650-7	439	37'	32'3"	11,800	390	Engine change. Serials 43–24752/901, 42–106739/978.
P-51C-1-3-NT	1360 h.p.-Packard V-1650-3	436	37'	32'3"	11,800	350	P-51B built in Dallas.
P-51C-10-NT	1450 h.p.-Packard V-1650-7	439	37'	32'3"	11,800	1400	Dallas-built P-51Bs w/ engine change. Serials 42–103329/978, 43–24902/25251, 44–10753/11152. 636 P-51Cs to Royal Air Force as Mustang III. 20 P-51Cs modified as F-6C-NT for USAAF.
P-51D-NA	1450 h.p.-Packard V-1650-7	437	37'	32'3"	12,100 (Max.)	6502	Bubble canopy. 6–.50-cal. machine guns. 281 P-51Ds to Royal Air Force as Mustang IV. 136 P-51Ds modified to F-6D-NA for USAAF. Serials 42–106539/540, 44–13253/15752, 44–63160/64159, 44–72027/75026.

Model	Engine	Top Speed MPH	Wing Span	Length	Loaded Weight Lbs.	Quan.	Remarks
P-51D-NT	1450 h.p.-Packard V-1650-7	437	37'	32'3"	12,100	1454	P-51D built in Dallas. Serials 44–11153/352, 44–84390/989, 45–11343/742.
TP-51D-NT	1450 h.p.-Packard V-1650-7	435	37'	32'3"	11,300	10	Fighter-trainer. Serials 44–84610/611, 45–11443/450.
XP-51F	1450 h.p.-Packard V-1650-7	466	37'	32'3"	9060	3	Lightweight version. 4–.50-cal. machine guns. Serials 43–43332/34.
XP-51G	1500 h.p.-Rolls-Royce Merlin 145	472	37'	32'3"	8885	2	Engine change and Aero Products prop. Serials 43–43335/36.
P-51H	1380 h.p.-Packard V-1650-9	487	37'	33'4"	11,500	555	Engine change. 2218 h.p. w/water injection. 6–.50-cal. machine guns. Serials 44–64160/714.
XP-51J	1500 h.p.-Allison V-1710-119	480+	37'	32'1"	9140	2	Engine change. 4–.50-cal. machine guns. Serials 44–76027/28.
P-51K-NT	1450 h.p.-Packard V-1650-7	437	37'	32'3"	12,100	1337	P-51D made in Dallas with Aero Products prop. 594 to Royal Air Force as Mustang IV. 163 modified to F-6D-NT for USAAF. Serials 44–11353/12852.
P-51M	1400 h.p.-Packard V-1650-9A	491	37'	33'4"	11,500	1	P-51H with engine change. Serial 45–11743.
XP-82	2–1400 h.p.-Packard V-1650-23/25	480	51'3"	38'1"	24,600	2	First Twin Mustangs. Serials 44–83886/887.
XP-82A	2–1500 h.p.-Allison V-1710-119	482	51'3"	38'1"	25,000	1	Engine change. Serial

Designation	Number	Weight	Height	Length	Engine	Remarks
P-82B	20	24,000	38'1"	51'3"	2–1400 h.p.-Packard V-1650-9	Production version of Twin Mustang. Serials 44–65160/179.
P-82C	(1)	25,000	38'1"	51'3"	2–1400 h.p.-Packard V-1650-23	10th P-82B for all-weather testing.
P-82D	(1)	25,000	38'1"	51'3"	2–1400 h.p.-Packard V-1650-23	P-82B for all-weather testing. Radar pod.
P-82E	100	24,900	39'	51'3"	2–1600 h.p.-Allison V-1710-143/145	P-82B with engine change. Serials 46–255/354.
P-82F	100	26,226	39'	51'3"	2–1600 h.p.-Allison V-1710-143/145	P-82E for all-weather fighting. Serials 46–405/504.
P-82G	50	26,000	39'	51'3"	2–1600 h.p.-Allison V-1710-143/145	With new and larger radar equipment. Serials 46–355/404.

MUSTANG COMBAT UNITS OF WORLD WAR II
U. S. ARMY AIR FORCES

1st Air Commando Group: Operated Mustang fighter squadrons within its India-based unit from February 1944 until May 1944. These P-51s bombed and strafed enemy airdromes and positions in addition to flying escort for bombers and cargo aircraft of the unit. The P-51s flew many sorties covering Wingate's invasion of Burma in March and April of 1944. Markings: Five diagonal white stripes around the fuselage, aft of the cockpit.

2nd Air Commando Group: Between November 1944 and May 1945, the Mustangs operating with this unit supported Allied forces by striking enemy airfields and transport from their bases in India. Flew support for cargo aircraft and were used as escort for bombers to targets in the vicinity of Rangoon. Did bombing in Thailand and flew reconnaissance missions.

3rd Air Commando Group: Fifth Air Force. Went into action in the Philippines in late 1944. Its Mustangs flew ground support and attacked enemy installations, particularly on Luzon. Escorted bombers to Formosa and the China coast. Made numerous fighter sweeps against airfields and rail targets on Formosa.

4th Fighter Group: Eighth Air Force. This unit, which was the old Eagle Squadron outfit, got its Mustangs in February 1944 and flew its first combat mission in them on the twenty-fifth. Flew many outstanding bomber-escort missions. On March 3, 1944, two flights of Mustangs routed more than 60 Luftwaffe fighters in the Berlin area, destroying six of them. The effect of the new Mustangs showed immediately. The unit destroyed 156 e/a in March 1944. On a mission to Brunswick on April 8, 1944, the P-51s shot down 31 Germans for the loss of four Mustangs. Led first shuttle mission from England to Russia on June 21, 1944. Completed many very successful strafing missions against German airfields in the spring of 1945. Markings: Red spinners and cowling. Sqdn. Code Letters: 334th F.S.-QP, 335th F.S.-WD, 336th F.S.-VF.

8th Reconnaissance Group: Used some F-6 Mustangs on photo and reconnaissance missions over Burma, China, French Indochina and Thailand during 1944. Also did some bombing and strafing in addition to bomber-escort duty.

10th Photo Reconnaissance Group: Ninth Air Force. Operated the first P-51A which had been fitted out as camera aircraft in England. Later utilized F-6 aircraft as a portion of the unit's command. These Mustangs did extensive visual- and photo-reconnaissance work until the end of the war in Europe. Sqdn. Code Letters: (There was considerable interchange of squadrons between the recce groups during the war. Listed here are codes of squadrons which flew with both the 10th and 67th Reconnaissance Groups.) 12th Sqdn.-ZM, 15th Sqdn.-5M, 107th Sqdn.-AX, 109th Sqdn.-VX.

15th Fighter Group: VII Fighter Command. Received P-51s in late 1944 and moved to Iwo Jima in February 1945. Supported the ground forces on the island during March 1945. Began strikes against airfields, shipping and installations on the other islands in the Bonins in late March. Flew its first very long range mission escorting the B-29s to Japan on April 7, 1945. The mission met with heavy opposition and the Mustangs of this unit were credited with destroying seventeen enemy fighters. Continued to escort the B-29s until they turned to night missions and then flew fighter sweeps over the Japanese home islands until the end of the war. Markings: 45th F.S.-Deep-green diagonal bands with narrow black borders on the wings, horizontal and vertical tail surfaces. Spinner from front was banded black, green and silver. 47th F.S.-Black stripes with narrow yellow bands on the wings, just outboard of the machine guns, on the horizontal tail and about the aft fuselage. On the vertical tail was an inverted black triangle, with narrow yellow bands. Spinner from front was banded yellow, black and yellow. 78th F.S.-Tips of the wings and horizontal and vertical tails painted yellow with a black band, of equal width, inboard or below the yellow. Spinner was painted all yellow and the forward part of the nose was black.

20th Fighter Group: Eighth Air Force. This unit converted to P-51s on July 17, 1944. Began Mustang operations on July 20 and drew first blood five days after the switchover when Lieutenants Moncrieff and Adams surprised and broke up a formation of fifty Me 109s over central Germany. After destroying three of them, they then attacked another formation of over fifty Me 109s and were able to make a getaway. Had outstanding strafing missions on August 25 and October 6 when thirty and forty German planes respectively were destroyed on the ground. Destroyed twenty-eight German fighters in the air while escorting the bombers to Merseburg on November 2, 1944. Fought off Me 262s while escorting bombers north of Berlin on April 10, 1945. Pilots of the unit credited with five of the jets. Markings: Alternate white and black stripes starting from the spinner and continuing to the aft engine cowling. Sqdn. Code Letters: 55th F.S.-KI, 77th F.S.-LC, 79th F.S.-MC.

21st Fighter Group: VII Fighter Command. Moved to Iwo Jima in Mustangs during February–March 1945. Sustained casualties during Japanese banzai charge on the night of March 26–27, but flew first combat mission the next day against airfield on Haha Jima. Won Distinguished Unit Citation for the first VLR escort mission with the B-29s on April 7, 1945. Continued to fly escort missions and, later, primarily fighter sweeps against the Japanese home islands until the end of the war. Markings: A horizontal band on the vertical tail, the wingtips and horizontal tailtips and the spinner being of a squadron color—Blue for the 46th F.S., yellow for the 72nd F.S. and white for the 531st F.S. A narrow black band bordered the color markings, while another was placed behind the spinner.

23rd Fighter Group: Fourteenth Air Force. The famed "Flying Tiger" Group flew its first P-51 mission on November 23, 1943, when it participated on the mission against the island of Formosa. In that attack, the pilots shot down five enemy fighters in the air and destroyed four on the ground. From December 1943 until April 1944 the group was primarily engaged in fighter sweeps, dive-bombing and strafing missions. The unit received a DUC for its action against Japanese ground forces during June 17–25, 1944, when the enemy launched an all-out attack down the Siang River valley in Hunan Province, China. Despite adverse weather and intense enemy ground fire, the Mustangs of the 23rd destroyed much enemy equipment and shipping and killed over 1600 troops. The group continued to support ground troops by attacking enemy-troop installations and to fly attacks against harbor facilities at Shanghai, Canton and Hong Kong to the end of the war.

27th Fighter-Bomber Group: Equipped with A-36s in North Africa where it joined the Twelfth Air Force in June of 1943. Flew dive-bombing and strafing missions against Pantelleria and supported ground forces in the invasion and conquest of Sicily. Provided air cover for the invasion of Italy at Salerno and received a DUC for their air attacks against German armored columns on September 10, 1943. Continued to support Fifth Army troops in their A-36s until June 1944 when the unit converted to P-47s.

31st Fighter Group: Converted from Spitfires to Mustangs when it joined the Fifteenth Air Force in Italy in April 1944. This unit scored 379 aerial victories flying the P-51 between this date and the end of the war. In their first month of Mustang operations the group won a DUC for their performance on April 21. On a mission to Ploesti, Rumania, a weather recall was given, but some of the bombers apparently didn't receive the message and continued to the target. The 31st went on to provide escort and broke up a massive attack of enemy fighters, destroying seventeen of them. The unit received a second DUC for their action during the Russian shuttle mission of 22–26 July 1944. On their second day in Russia they flew a mission over the German-Polish front lines where they encountered a bevy of e/a and destroyed thirty of them in the air and a further thirteen on the ground. During the shuttle mission the 31st shot down thirty-seven enemy aircraft and lost none of their own. The last real "big" mission for the unit was the trip to Berlin on March 24, 1945 which saw the 31st tangle with the German Me 262 jets and in the encounter shot five of them from the sky without a loss of their own. Markings: Red spinners and diagonal red and white stripes on the vertical tail. Sqdn. Code Letters: 307th F.S.-MX, 308th F.S.-HL, 309th F.S.-WZ.

35th Fighter Group: Fifth Air Force. This veteran unit received P-51s while stationed on Luzon in the Philippine Islands in March of 1945. Flew numerous ground-support operations as well as fighter sweeps and bomber-escort missions to Formosa and China. Moved to Okinawa in June of 1945. Flew several fighter sweeps over Kyushu and missions to Korea and the China coast before V-J Day.

52nd Fighter Group: This ex-Spitfire unit received its P-51s in April and May 1944 when it was assigned to the Fifteenth Air Force in Italy. From May until the end of the war, the unit's Mustangs ranged over Germany, Austria, Czechoslovakia and the Balkans to provide escort for the heavy bombers. On June 9, 1944, their Mustangs provided superior escort to a scattered bomber stream attacking targets at Munich, Germany, and broke up successive concentrations of enemy fighters. In the running air battle, fourteen German fighters were shot down without the loss of a single P-51. A highly successful strafing mission was flown by the group on August 31, 1944, when they strafed Reghin landing ground in Rumania. Despite aerial opposition and ground flak, the Mustangs of the 52nd managed to wreak havoc by destroying sixty airplanes on the ground while the top cover downed nine of the intercepting aircraft. Markings: Red spinners and yellow aft fuselage and tail surfaces.

55th Fighter Group: Eighth Air Force. This group converted to Mustangs from P-38s on July 14, 1944. They were not long in displaying their prowess in the new craft as is exemplified by their record between September 3 and 13, 1944. In addition to escorting bombers and breaking up concentrations of enemy fighters they went down and wrecked Luftwaffe airdromes on the way home. During the ten-day period they destroyed 106 enemy aircraft in the air and on the ground. On February 19, 1945, its proficiency as a strafing unit was further demonstrated when the Mustangs went down to the deck to destroy eighty-one locomotives. The following day they broke their own record when they chalked up eighty-nine locomotives. Markings: Spinner from front banded green, yellow and green. Two bands of green-and-yellow checks aft of the spinner. Sqdn. Code Letters: 38th F.S.-CG, 338th F.S.-CL, 343rd F.S.-CY.

67th Tactical Reconnaissance Group: Ninth Air Force. Operated a number of squadrons at various periods of time that utilized P-51 and F-6 aircraft. Did excellent work on a wide variety of photo recce, visual recce, weather recce and bomb-damage-assessment missions. Mustangs of this unit also took their toll of enemy aircraft when they encountered them in the course of their mission.

68th Tactical Reconnaissance Group: Used some Mustangs for photo- and visual-reconnaissance missions from its bases in Italy. These aircraft ranged over France, Germany, Austria and the Balkans.

69th Tactical Reconnaissance Group: Ninth Air Force. Began operations in F-6s in March 1945. Flew visual- and photo-recce missions up to V-E Day. Sqdn. Code Letters: 10th Sqdn. YC, 22nd Sqdn.-QL.

71st Tactical Reconnaissance Group: Fifth Air Force. Received some P-51s and F-6s in late 1944. Flew many missions over the Philippines, Formosa and China. Maj. William Shomo won the Congressional Medal of Honor flying one of its Mustangs on January 11, 1945, when he encountered and shot down seven enemy planes while on a visual-reconnaissance mission.

78th Fighter Group: Last Eighth Air Force fighter group to convert to P-51s. Received its first Mustangs in late December 1944. Its fighters did excellent strafing work in the spring of 1945. On April 10, 1945, they destroyed fifty-two e/a on an airfield in Czechoslovakia and six days later they went back to another Czech airfield and racked up a record total of 135 planes destroyed and eighty-nine damaged on the ground. Markings: Black-and-white-checkerboard cowling. Sqdn. Code Letters: 82nd F.S.-MX, 83rd F.S.-HL, 84th F.S.-WZ.

86th Fighter-Bomber Group: Twelfth Air Force. Flew many dive-bombing and strafing missions in its A-36s which it received in North Africa in July of 1943. Supported ground forces in Sicily and at Salerno during the invasion of Italy.

311th Fighter Group: Tenth Air Force. Began operations in A-36s and P-51s late in 1943. While based in India its Mustangs flew many bomber-escort and ground-support missions. In July 1944 the unit moved to Burma where it gave excellent cover to Allied ground forces. The group moved to China in August 1944 and was used primarily as bomber escort up to the end of the war.

325th Fighter Group: Fifteenth Air Force. Received P-51s in May 1944 and was selected as the Mustang group to escort bombers on the first shuttle mission to Russia from Italy on June 2, 1941. The unit scored many aerial victories while flying cover for the heavies, but they also excelled in strafing. On September 8, 1944, they attacked two landing fields in Yugoslavia and of the 106 aircraft parked on the fields only five escaped destruction. One flight from the unit intercepted a force of forty-eight Luftwaffe fighters attacking the bombers on the afternoon of October 16, 1944, and shot nine of them down. The bombers returned unscathed. Their last big air battle took place on March 14, 1945, when the unit's Mustangs took on thirty-eight FW 190s over Hungary and shot seventeen of them down. Markings: Red spinners and black-and-yellow-checkerboard tail surfaces.

332nd Fighter Group: Fifteenth Air Force. The last fighter group of the Fifteenth AF to receive Mustangs. Began its P-51 operations in June of 1944. Primarily engaged in bomber-escort missions, but also flew some highly successful strafing raids in the Balkans. This all-Negro unit won a DUC when it fought off German jets attacking the bombers on a mission to Berlin on March 24, 1945. Markings: Red spinners and tail surfaces.

339th Fighter Group: Eighth Air Force. This unit arrived in England in March of 1944 and began its operations by flying a sweep in its P-51s on April 30, 1944. On September 11, 1944, its Mustangs attacked 100-plus

German fighters which were queuing up to intercept the bombers. In the air battle which followed, fifteen of the enemy were destroyed. The same day, one squadron of the group strafed an airfield near Karlsruhe and destroyed twenty planes on the ground. This unit also flew some very successful Me 262 suppression missions in early 1945, destroying a number of them in the air and many on the ground. In a year of combat, the 339th destroyed 239½ c/a in the air and 440½ e/a on the ground. Markings: Spinner from the front banded white, red and white. Sqdn. Code Letters: 503rd. F.S.-D7, 504th F.S.-6N, 505th F.S.-5Q.

352nd Fighter Group: Eighth Air Force. Gave up its P-47s for Mustangs on April 7, 1944. On May 8, 1944, intercepted 100-plus enemy fighters attacking the bomber stream in the vicinity of Bremen. Shot down twenty-seven planes in the air battle that ranged from 23,000 feet to the deck. Shot down thirty-eight e/a attacking the bombers in the Dresden area on November 2, 1944. 487th Squadron downed twenty-three e/a attacking their airdrome at Asch, Belgium, on New Year's Day 1945. Markings: Blue spinners and cowling. Sqdn. Code Letters: 328th F.S.-PE, 486th F.S.-PZ, 487th F.S.-HO.

353rd Fighter Group: Eighth Air Force. Converted from P-47s to P-51s on September 30, 1944. Gave invaluable support to the bombers on missions deep into Germany, and destroyed many enemy aircraft on strafing missions on the way home. Its greatest Mustang air victory came when its aircraft were on patrol west of Kassel on March 24, 1945. Several gaggles of Me 109s and FW 190s were engaged and the unit's P-51s destroyed twenty-nine of them. Markings: Spinner from the front banded black, yellow, black and yellow. Black-and-yellow-checkerboard cowling. Sqdn. Code Letters: 350th F.S.-LH, 351st F.S.-YJ, 352nd F.S.-SX.

354th Fighter Group: Ninth Air Force. The "Pioneer Mustang" group in the ETO. Began its operations in December 1943. Flew many of its early missions as escort for Eighth AF bombers. The unit's first big victory came on January 5, 1944, when the Mustangs downed eighteen e/a while escorting the bombers to Kiel. Maj. James H. Howard won the Congressional Medal of Honor for breaking up large enemy fighter force on mission to Halberstadt on January 11, 1944. Moved to France in the summer of 1944 and flew many ground-support as well as fighter-sweep missions. Converted to P-47s for brief period; November 1944–February 1945. Scored over six hundred confirmed victories flying Mustangs. Markings: 353rd F.S.-White spinners, blue triangles on white noseband. 355th F.S.-Blue spinners, blue-and-white-checkerboard noseband. 356th F.S.-White spinners, white stars on blue noseband. Sqdn. Code Letters: 353rd F.S.-FT, 355th F.S.-GQ, 356th F.S.-AJ.

355th Fighter Group: Eighth Air Force. Went operational in Mustangs on March 3, 1944, after flying P-47s. Despite a furious snow squall the unit went down to strafe enemy airdromes on April 5, 1944. In a furious forty-minute attack the P-51s destroyed forty-three planes on the ground and shot eight out of the air. Continued to provide bomber escort and to strafe enemy installations until V-E Day. Markings: White spinner and yellow noseband. Sqdn. Code Letters: 354th F.S.-WR, 357th F.S.-OS, 358th F.S.-YF.

356th Fighter Group: Eighth Air Force. Converted to P-51s on November 6, 1944. Flew many combat missions as escort to the bombers and ground attacks against enemy airfields and installations up to the end of the war. Markings: Red-and-blue-striped spinner bands. Blue diamonds on red cowling. Sqdn. Code Letters: 359th F.S.-OC, 360th F.S.-PI, 361st F.S.-QI.

357th Fighter Group: Eighth Air Force. Another group that flew Mustangs from the beginning. Entered operations on February 10, 1944. Received a DUC for their outstanding performance on the first heavy-bomber mission to Berlin on March 6, 1944. The unit tackled terrific enemy opposition, broke up their attacks and downed twenty of them, losing none of their own. On January 14, 1945, the group fought one of the longest and most fierce air battles to take place in the ETO. In a conflict that lasted over thirty minutes the Mustangs downed fifty-six e/a for a loss of only three P-51s. This unit is credited with 609½ aerial victories flying P-51s. Markings: Spinner from the front banded red, yellow and red. Two red-and-yellow-checkered nosebands. Sqdn. Code Letters: 362nd F.S.-G4, 363rd F.S.-B6, 364th F.S.-C5.

359th Fighter Group: Eighth Air Force. Converted to P-51s on May 4, 1944. Had an outstanding day while escorting bombers on September 11, 1944. Broke up the attack of fifty-plus enemy fighters in the vicinity of Gissen and then went down to engage more fighters taking off from Gotha airdrome. Destroyed five in the air and another four on the ground. Fought off three more gaggles of Luftwaffe fighters attempting to get to the bombers, shooting down more enemy planes. Destroyed seven locomotives on the way home. Total for the day was thirty-five e/a destroyed in the air and on the ground. Supported the airborne invasion of Holland later that month and flew support missions for the Rhine crossing in March 1945. Markings: Green spinners and cowling. Sqdn. Code Letters: 368th F.S.-CV, 369th F.S.-IV, 370th F.S.-CS.

361st Fighter Group: Converted to Mustangs on July 28, 1944. Flew many bomber-escort missions. Went to Belgium in December 1944 to fly support during the Battle of the Bulge. Did extensive strafing work in the spring of 1945. Markings: Yellow spinner and noseband. Sqdn. Code Letters: 374th F.S.-B7, 375th F.S.-E2, 376th F.S.-E9.

363rd Fighter Group: Ninth Air Force. Arrived in England in December 1943 and began operations flying Mustangs in January 1944. Flew numerous bomber-escort missions and supported the invasion of France with bombing and strafing missions. Became a Tactical Reconnaissance Group in September 1944. Flew photo- and visual-recce missions up to the end of the war. Sqdn. Code Letters: 160th T.R.S.-A9, 161st T.R.S.-B3, 162nd T.R.S.-C3. (As fighter squadrons they were designated 380th, 381st and 382nd. Code letters were the same, respectively.)

364th Fighter Group: Eighth Air Force. Converted to P-51s on July 28, 1944. Flew escort, dive-bombing, strafing and patrol missions. Turned in an outstanding performance while escorting the heavies to Frankfurt on December 27, 1944. One squadron attacked gaggles of German fighters in the vicinity of Coblenz, shooting down ten of them and breaking up the attack. A second squadron shot down eight out of a gaggle of fifteen to twenty FW 190s. The third squadron attacked a formation of thirty FW 190s and destroyed ten of them. Collectively the group had destroyed twenty-eight e/a for the loss of one Mustang. Markings: White spinner. Blue-and-white-striped noseband. Sqdn. Code Letters: 383rd F.S.-N2, 384th F.S.-5Y, 385th F.S.-5E.

370th Fighter Group: Ninth Air Force. Converted to P-51s in February–March 1945. Bombed bridges and docks in support of the Rhine River crossing. Supported ground operations in the Ruhr Valley. Markings: 401st F.S.-Yellow spinner and horizontal band on vertical tail. 402nd F.S.-Blue spinner and diagonal band on vertical tail. 485th F.S.-Red spinner and vertical band on vertical tail. Sqdn. Code Letters: 401st F.S.-7F, 402nd F.S.-E6, 485th F.S.-9D.

479th Fighter Group: Eighth Air Force. Converted to P-51s on September 27, 1944. Had first real big day flying Mustangs on December 5, 1944. Intercepted a big gaggle of German fighters north of Berlin and shot fourteen of them down. On Christmas Day, 1944, the group had three good scraps and downed twenty-three Luftwaffe fighters. Did excellent strafing work on airfields during March and April 1945. Markings: Natural metal. Squadron colors on rudders only markings used. Squadron Code Letters: 434th F.S.-L2, 435th F.S.-J2, 436th F.S.-B9.

506th Fighter Group: VII Fighter Command. Flew its first missions from Iwo Jima against the Bonin Islands on May 18, 1945. Participated in several of the VLR escort missions with the B-29s in June of 1945. Markings: 457th F.S.-Red tails. 458th F.S.-Diagonal zebra stripes on tail. 462nd F.S.-Yellow tails.

The 3rd and 5th Fighter Groups of the Chinese-American Composite Wing also operated a number of Mustangs in 1944–45. The exact dates of the P-51 operations are not known.

TOP AAF MUSTANG SCORERS—WORLD WAR II

Name	AF	Group	P-51 Score	Total WWII Score
Maj. George Preddy	8	352	23.83	26.83
Lt. Col. J. C. Meyer	8	352	21.	24.
Capt. J. J. Voll	15	31	21.	21.
Capt. R. S. Wetmore	8	359	20.	22.6
Maj. Leonard K. Carson	8	357	18.5	18.5
Lt. Col. Glenn T. Eagleston	9	354	18.5	18.5
Lt. Col. John C. Herbst	14	23	18.	18.
Maj. John B. England	8	357	17.5	17.5
Capt. Henry W. Brown	8	355	17.2	17.2
Maj. Robert W. Foy	8	357	17.	17.
Capt. James S. Varnell	15	52	17.	17.
Capt. C. E. Anderson, Jr.	8	357	16.5	16.5
Capt. John F. Thornell	8	352	16.25	17.25
Maj. Donald M. Beerbower	9	354	15.5	15.5
Maj. R. A. Peterson	8	357	15.5	15.5
Lt. Col. Jack T. Bradley	9	354	15.	15.
Maj. Samuel J. Brown	15	31	15.	15.

MUSTANGS WITH THE RAF
MARKS I, IA AND II

2 Squadron: Received some of the first Mustangs in mid-1942. Became operational flying photo-reconnaissance missions in November 1942. Flew all three Marks up until mid-November 1944. Sqdn. Code Letters: XV.

4 Squadron: Received a sprinkling of Mustangs in May 1942 for reconnaissance missions. By early 1943 was largely Mustang equipped. Converted to Spitfires in late 1943. Sqdn. Code Letters: TV.

16 Squadron: Received first Mustangs in April 1942. Operational with the craft on photo reconnaissance until September 1943. Sqdn. Code Letters: UG.

26 Squadron: Received Mustangs gradually from February 1942 until operational in July 1942. Flew many missions over the Continent on a series of tours up until late 1943. Operational in Mustang Is again in October 1944, flying many photo missions over V-2 sites in France. Sqdn. Code Letters: RM, later XC.

63 Squadron: Utilized Mustang I and IAs for many missions over the Continent between June 1943 and February 1944 while assigned to Army Co-operation Command. Sqdn. Code Letters: NE, later UB.

No. 116 Squadron: Used a few Mustang Is for radar calibration work. No operations.

168 Squadron: Operated Mustang Mark Is and IAs from December 1942 until October 1944. Went to France with Second Tactical Air Force in June 1944 and flew missions from a number of advanced airstrips.

225 Squadron: Borrowed four F-6Bs from USAAF for photo operation during April and May 1943 during the Tunisian campaign.

239 Squadron: Flew Mustangs from May 1942 until October 1943. This unit took part in many photo, recce and strafing operations over occupied Europe during this period. Sqdn. Code Letters: HB.

169 Squadron: Formed in June 1942 for Mustang intruder operations. Flew many railway and coastal strafing missions, primarily over Holland. Converted to Mosquitoes in late 1943. Sqdn. Code Letters: VI.

241 Squadron: Received Mustangs in the spring of 1942 but never became operational in them.

260 Squadron: Received a few Mustang Is for transition training in March 1944.

268 Squadron: This tactical-reconnaissance unit utilized some Mustang Mark Is and IAs from June 1942 until the end of the war. Operated from bases in France, Belgium and Holland late in the conflict. Sqdn. Code Letters: NM.

309 Squadron: Flew anti-shipping missions utilizing Mustangs from December 1942 until February 1944. Sqdn. Code Letters: WC.

400 Squadron: This RCAF unit operated some Mustangs on photo-reconnaissance missions from November 1942 until March 1944.

414 Squadron: Received Mustang Is in early summer 1942 and entered combat in August. Scored 1st Mustang victory while covering the Dieppe raid on August 19, 1942. Continued to fly Mustangs until June 1944. Sqdn. Code Letters: RU.

430 Squadron: Became operational with Mustangs in late May 1943. Flew many missions over France before and during the invasion in 1944. Moved to the Continent in July 1944 and continued to operate Mustang Is until December 1944.

516 Squadron: Formed as a transport squadron in Scotland in April 1943. Operated a few Mustang Is and IAs until early 1944.

613 Squadron: Flew Mustang Is from March 1943 until December 1943. Sqdn. Code Letters: SY.

MARKS III AND IV

19 Squadron: Mustang operations started in February 1944, with fighter sweeps and escorts to U.S. bombers. Flew numerous anti-shipping escorts. Saw extensive action in support of the Normandy beachhead in June 1944. Moved to France for ground-support duties but returned to U.K. in late September 1944. On September 30, 1944, escorted Lancasters on first daylight mission over the Ruhr. Continued to fly sweeps and escort missions until the end of the war in Europe. Sqdn. Code Letters: QV.

64 Squadron: Received Mustangs in December 1944 and began flying bomber-escort missions in them at once. Flew cover for numerous Lancaster daylight missions and on January 14, 1945, intercepted and shot down eight enemy aircraft. Sqdn. Code Letters: SH.

65 Squadron: Flew the first of many escort missions on February 15, 1944. They blooded their Mustangs over Nancy on April 22 and on a sweep to Aalborg, Denmark, heavy enemy opposition was encountered and the Mustangs accounted for nine of them. Began dive bombing in May 1944 and continued this type of ground-support missions during and after the invasion of France. Moved to France on June 26, 1944, and continued to support the Allied armies at various advanced strips up to October 1944. Sqdn. Code Letters: YT.

118 Squadron: Received Mustangs in December 1944 and began escort operations in February 1945. Flew cover for Lancaster missions until the end of the war. Sqdn. Code Letters: NK.

112 Squadron: Flew Mark III and IV Mustangs on ground-support operation in Italy from the summer of 1944 until May 1945. Also flew a number of missions over Yugoslavia. Sqdn. Code Letters: GA.

122 Squadron: Began bomber-escort mission flying Mustangs in February 1944. Flew cover for U.S. bombers to Berlin in March 1944. Caught eight He 111s coming into Dole/Tavaux airfield on April 23, 1944, and shot six of them down. Operated over the invasion area in June 1944 and moved to France late that month. Flew missions in support of ground troops from airstrips on the Continent until September 1944. Did exceptional work during the Arnheim paratroop drop in Holland in September. Became bomber escort until after return to U.K. Sqdn. Code Letters: MT.

126 Squadron: This unit's Mustangs began escorting the Lancaster bombers in January 1945. While flying cover for the heavies on April 9, 1945, on a mission to the U-boat works at Hamburg, it met and beat off an attack of twelve-plus Me 262 jets, destroying one of them. Sqdn. Code Letters: 5J.

129 Squadron: Initial Mustang escort operations began in April 1944, but did not see aerial combat until D-day when an FW 190 was shot down. Flew anti-V-1 missions from July until September 1944. Supported the Arnheim operation in September and escorted Lancasters, Halifaxes and Mosquitoes up to the end of the war. Sqdn. Code Letters: DV.

165 Squadron: Received Mustangs in January 1945 and began bomber-escort operations immediately. F/O Haslops downed an Me 163 while covering the bombers on a mission to Leipzig on April 10, 1945. Sqdn. Code Letters: SK.

213 Squadron: Received one flight of Mustangs while based in Egypt in June 1944. Fully equipped with Mustangs after move to Italy in July 1944. Flew many missions over Yugoslavia and Greece. Caught He 111s towing Go 242 gliders over Belgrade on September 8, 1944; shot down the two He 111s and destroyed the gliders in the air and on the ground. Flew Mark IIIs and Mark IVs up to the end of the war. Sqdn. Code Letters: AK.

234 Squadron: Utilized Mustangs for escort missions and fighter sweeps from the fall of 1944 until April 1945. Ended the war escorting Mosquitoes and Beaufighters over Denmark and Norway. Sqdn. Code Letters: AZ.

249 Squadron: Flew Mustangs with the Balkan Air Force from October 1944 until mid-April 1945. Majority of missions were fighter sweeps and ground strafing over the Balkans and Greece. Sqdn. Code Letters: GN.

260 Squadron: In mid-March 1944, became the first RAF unit in Italy to receive Mustangs. Flew ground-support and bomber-escort missions to Yugoslavia. In February 1945, began using rockets for ground operations. Sqdn. Code Letters: HS.

303 Squadron: This Polish unit didn't receive Mustangs until April 1945. Flew a few escort missions in them before V-E Day. Sqdn. Code Letters: RF.

306 Squadron: Began flying fighter sweeps in their Mustangs in April 1944. Saw first combat on June 7, 1944, when these Polish pilots tangled with over thirty enemy fighters in the Beuzeville area of France. They destroyed five of the enemy, plus three probables. From late June 1944 until September 1944 the squadron was on anti-V-1 duty. Supported the Arnheim drop over Holland and then resumed escort duties to the end of the war. S/Ldr. J. Zulikowski credited with an Me 262 on April 9, 1945, while escorting Lancasters to Hamburg. Sqdn. Code Letters: UZ.

309 Squadron: This was another Polish unit which began bomber-escort operations with its Mark III Mustangs in December 1944. While escorting Lancasters to Hamburg on April 9, 1945, it intercepted and beat off an attack from eight Me 262s, destroying three and damaging two of them in the fight. Sqdn. Code Letters: WC.

315 Squadron: A Polish unit which received its first Mustangs in April 1944. Began bomber-escort missions later the same month. Participated in many bombing and ground-support missions in the invasion area during June 1944. Flew anti-V-1 missions in July 1944. While escorting torpedo Beaufighters on July 30, 1944, encountered fifteen enemy fighters and shot down eight of them with no losses. Engaged sixty-plus FW 190s in the Beauvais area on August 18, 1944, and shot down sixteen of them, but lost one Mustang—S/Ldr. Horbaczewski. Shot down five enemy fighters on Beaufighter-escort mission to Norway on December 17, 1944. Continued to escort heavy bombers over Germany until the end of the war. Sqdn. Code Letters: SZ.

316 Squadron: The Mustangs which were received in April 1944, by this Polish squadron were used primarily for convoy patrol up until July 1944, when they went on Anti-V-1 duty. They returned to sea duty in September 1944 and then flew a number of sweeps over Denmark. At the end of October 1944 they began bomber-escort duties for the Lancasters and Halifaxes. Sqdn. Code Letters: PK.

442 Squadron: Mustang IVs received in April 1945. Flew a few escort missions in the craft before the end of hostilities. Sqdn. Code Letters: Y2.

611 Squadron: Converted to Mustangs in mid-March 1945. Escorted Lancasters and Halifaxes over Germany until the end of the war. Shot down five FW 190s in the Berlin area on April 16, 1945. Sqdn. Code Letters: FY.

3 RAAF Squadron: This Italian-based Australian unit operated Mustang Mark IIIs and IVs from November 1944 until V-E Day. The majority of its missions were in ground support in northern Italy and on fighter sweeps over Yugoslavia. Sqdn. Code Letters: CV.

5 SAAF Squadron: A South African unit which converted to Mustangs in October 1944. Flew ground-support missions from its Italian base up to the end of the war.

LEADING RAF MUSTANG SCORERS

S/Ldr. E. Horbaczewski, DSO, DFC	315 Sqdn.	5.5
S/Ldr. L. A. P. Burra-Robinson, DFC	122, 65 Sqdns.	5.25
Sgt. J. Bargielowski, DFM	315 Sqdn.	5.
S/Ldr. H. Pietrzak, DFC	306, 315 Sqdns.	4.85
F/O B. Vassiliades, DFM	19 Sqdn.	4.85
F/Lt. B. G. Collyns, DFC	65, 19 Sqdns.	3.5
W/Cdr. G. R. A. McG. Johnston, DSO, DFC		3.5
W/Cdr. W. Christie, DSO, DFC		3.

LEADING RAF MUSTANG V-1 SCORERS

F/O J. Hartley	129 Sqdn.	11.
F/Lt. D. F. Ruchwaldy	129 Sqdn.	10.
F/Sgt. S. Rudowski	306 Sqdn.	9.5
F/Sgt. S. Siekierski	306 Sqdn.	9.
F/Sgt. J. Zalenski	306 Sqdn.	8.5
W/O T. Szymanski	316 Sqdn.	8.
F/Lt. R. G. Kleinmayer	129 Sqdn.	7.5
F/Sgt. A. Pietrzak	316 Sqdn.	7.
F/Sgt. T. Jankowski	315 Sqdn.	6.85

FRENCH AIR FORCE

2/33 Tactical Reconnaissance Squadron: Began operations flying F-6C and F-6D aircraft in January of 1945. Did photo survey of the Rhine for French forces. Performed tactical-reconnaissance work for the French First Army after the crossing of the Rhine. Sqdn. Code Letters: R7.

MUSTANG UNITS IN KOREA

8th Fighter-Bomber Group: August 1950–December 1950

18th Fighter-Bomber Group: July 1950–January 1953

35th Fighter-Interceptor Group: July 1950–May 1951

49th Fighter-Bomber Group: June 1950–September 1951

67th Tactical Reconnaissance Group operated some RF-51s.

68th Fighter All-Weather Squadron flew F-82s over Korea, June 1950.

339th Fighter All-Weather Squadron operated F-82s over Korea in June 1950.

No. 77 Royal Australian Air Force Squadron flew Mustangs from July 1950 to April 1951.

No. 2 South African Air Force Squadron operated Mustangs from November 1950 to January 1953.

INDEX